UFOs OVER BONNYBRIDGE:

Unraveling the Secrets of the Falkirk Triangle

DJ BROWNE

Copyright © 2024 DJ Browne

All rights reserved.

ISBN:9798876825827

DEDICATION

To the multiple witnesses in and around central Scotland who deserve answers, I dedicate this book to you all, for your honesty, bravery and belief that one day the truth will be revealed about your encounters. And especially to my late grandmother – a Falkirk girl born and breed – who started my UFO journey in the 1960s.

CONTENTS

	Acknowledgments	i
1	THE EMERENCE	1
2	BONNYBRDGE FROM INDUSTRIAL HUB TO UFO HOTSPOT	3
3	INDUSTRIAL ROOTS & LANDSCAPE TRANSFORMATION	6
4	THE BIRTH OF BONNYBRIDGE UFO SIGHTINGS	12
5	THE FALKIRK TRIANGLE & OTHER WORLDWIDE HOTS SPOTS	32
6	GOVERNMENT INVOLVEMENT	66
7	SKEPTICISM, DEBUNKING, TRUTH & THE LEGACY	86

ACKNOWLEDGMENTS

Thanks to all those who contributed to this book – too many to mention by name alone. You know who you are. Big thanks.

CHAPTER ONE

The Emergence

In the quiet town of Bonnybridge, nestled amidst the picturesque landscapes of Scotland, an extraordinary tale unfolds. As the sun sets over the quaint streets and rolling hills, a mysterious phenomenon begins to captivate the collective imagination of the townsfolk. This phenomenon, etched into the very fabric of Bonnybridge's history, marks the genesis of a saga that transcends the ordinary and propels the town into the annals of the unexplained.

It all started innocently enough, as the residents of Bonnybridge began to notice peculiar occurrences in the skies above. Strange lights danced across the horizon, defying conventional explanations and sparking a sense of wonder mixed with trepidation. W1hispers of unidentified flying objects (UFOs) circulated through the community, giving rise to a shared curiosity that transcended age, occupation, and background.

The phenomenon gained momentum, gradually becoming a focal point of conversation in local cafes, town halls, and living rooms. With over a staggering 60,000 reported accounts of strange encounters in Central Scotland, the Falkirk Triangle is officially the number 1 hotspot for UFO/UAP sightings in the world. Witnesses came forward, recounting their inexplicable experiences with a mix of awe and uncertainty. Some spoke of eerie encounters with otherworldly beings, while others shared tales of inexplicably disrupted technology in the presence of these celestial enigmas.

As the anecdotal evidence accumulated, Bonnybridge found itself thrust into the spotlight of the broader UFO phenomenon. Sceptics and believers alike converged on the town, seeking to unravel the mysteries hidden within its skies. The otherwise serene town became a hotbed of speculation, drawing the attention of researchers, journalists, and enthusiasts eager to delve into the uncharted realms of the extraordinary.

This book seeks to navigate the uncharted territory of Bonnybridge's UFO encounters, unravelling the layers of mystery that shroud this small Scottish town. As we embark on this journey, I will explore the historical context, interview witnesses, and sift through the enigmatic clues that may provide insight into the otherworldly occurrences that have forever left an indelible mark on Bonnybridge's identity. Join me as I unravel the enigma in the sky, peeling back the layers of uncertainty to expose the extraordinary tales that lie hidden in the heart of the Falkirk Triangle that is Bonnybridge, Scotland.

CHAPTER TWO

Bonnybridge: from Industrial Hub to UFO Hotspot

Nestled in the heart of Scotland, Bonnybridge has a rich and varied history that spans centuries, evolving from its humble beginnings to becoming known as an unexpected hub for UFO sightings. This chapter delves into the early days of Bonnybridge, tracing its journey from an industrial centre to a location of fascination for both historians and UFO enthusiasts alike.

Bonnybridge's history can be traced back to the medieval period, with its name likely originating from the Old Scots words "bonnie" meaning pretty or beautiful, and "brigg" meaning bridge. The presence of a bridge suggests that the area was strategically important even in its early days, likely serving as a crossing point for travellers and traders.

As the centuries passed, Bonnybridge evolved into a thriving industrial hub during the 18th and 19th centuries. The construction of the Forth and Clyde Canal in the late 18th century played a pivotal role in the town's industrial growth, facilitating the transportation of goods and providing a vital link between the east and west coasts of Scotland. The canal brought economic prosperity to Bonnybridge, attracting industries such as ironworks, foundries, and mills. The availability of water and coal resources further fuelled the industrial expansion, turning Bonnybridge into a bustling centre of manufacturing and commerce.

The landscape of Bonnybridge, once dominated by agricultural fields and quaint villages, transformed into a landscape dotted with factories and chimneys, reflecting the Industrial Revolution's impact on the region. The growing population led to the development of infrastructure, including housing for workers and amenities such as schools and churches. The town's skyline changed, echoing the clatter of machinery and the rhythmic sounds of progress.

However, as with many industrial centres, Bonnybridge experienced challenges and fluctuations in its economic fortunes. The decline of traditional industries in the mid-20th century brought about significant changes, leading to the closure of factories and the loss of jobs. The town faced a period of adaptation, as residents sought new ways to sustain their livelihoods.

Amidst these shifts, Bonnybridge began to gain an unexpected reputation for something beyond its industrial past. In the late 20th century, the town became increasingly known for an unusual phenomenon — a surge in reported UFO sightings. The once-thriving industrial landscape became a backdrop for mysterious lights and unidentified flying objects, capturing the attention of locals and the wider public alike.

Beyond its historical narrative, Bonnybridge's landscape and culture contribute to the unique character of the town. The surrounding countryside offers picturesque views, with rolling hills and the meandering course of the Forth and Clyde Canal providing a serene contrast to the industrial remnants of the past.

Bonnybridge's architecture reflects the various stages of its development, with a blend of historic structures and more modern buildings. The town's layout has evolved over time, influenced by the needs of its changing population and industries. Streets that once echoed with the sounds of horse-drawn carts and factory workers now accommodate modern traffic, creating a tapestry that weaves together the past and present.

Cultural identity in Bonnybridge is shaped by a mix of traditional Scottish heritage and the resilience forged during periods of economic change. Local festivals and events celebrate the town's history, bringing together residents to share in their collective identity. The echoes of industrial labour are remembered through landmarks and museums, preserving the stories of those who shaped Bonnybridge's past.

As Bonnybridge gained notoriety for UFO sightings, the cultural landscape underwent a subtle shift. UFO enthusiasts and researchers flocked to the town, contributing to a unique subculture that blends local history with extra-terrestrial intrigue. The town, once primarily known for its industrial prowess, found itself thrust into the limelight of paranormal discussions.

Despite the UFO phenomenon drawing attention, Bonnybridge retains its charm as a community with a deep connection to its roots. Local businesses, traditional pubs, and community events continue to thrive, providing a sense of continuity and stability amidst the curiosity surrounding extra-terrestrial encounters.

Bonnybridge's journey from an industrial hub to a UFO hotspot is a fascinating narrative that intertwines economic shifts, cultural evolution, and the unexpected twists of paranormal intrigue. The landscape and culture of the town stand as a testament to the resilience of its residents and the multifaceted nature of its history. Bonnybridge remains a place where the past and present coexist, inviting exploration into the layers of its rich and diverse heritage.

CHAPTER THREE

Industrial Roots & Landscape Transformation

The 18th century marked a significant turning point in the history of Bonnybridge, a small town that would go on to play a pivotal role in the Industrial Revolution. This era, characterized by profound societal and economic changes, witnessed the emergence of Bonnybridge as a key player in Britain's industrial landscape. The transformation of Bonnybridge's once serene and pastoral surroundings was primarily driven by the establishment of mills and factories that harnessed the power of the Bonny Water river, propelling the town into the forefront of the industrial revolution.

Bonnybridge's landscape underwent a radical transformation during the Industrial Revolution as mills and factories sprang up along the banks of the Bonny Water river. The strategic utilization of this water resource enabled the town to power machinery, facilitating the mechanization of various industrial processes. The rhythmic hum of machinery replaced the tranquillity of the countryside, signalling Bonnybridge's irreversible shift towards industrialization.

Natural resources played a crucial role in this metamorphosis, with the abundance of coal and iron in the region becoming the bedrock of Bonnybridge's industrialization. The coal mines provided a steady supply of fuel for the burgeoning industries, while iron ore became a fundamental raw material for the production of goods ranging from machinery to infrastructure. These resources not only ignited the industrial engines but also laid the foundation for the town's economic prosperity.

Situated along the Forth and Clyde Canal, Bonnybridge gained prominence not only as an industrial centre but also as a vital transportation hub. The canal, a waterway that connected the east and west coasts of Scotland, facilitated the movement of goods and raw materials to and from Bonnybridge. This connectivity was instrumental in integrating the town into the broader economic currents of the time, enabling it to exchange resources and products with other industrial centres.

The Forth and Clyde Canal, traversing through the heart of Bonnybridge, became a lifeline for the town's economic activities. It not only linked Bonnybridge to other key industrial regions but also opened up avenues for trade and commerce, contributing significantly to the town's prosperity. The canal's role in transporting goods and fostering economic exchange further solidified Bonnybridge's status as a dynamic and interconnected industrial hub.

The Industrial Revolution brought about a profound change in Bonnybridge's social fabric. The influx of workers seeking employment in the burgeoning industries led to a population boom, transforming Bonnybridge from a small rural community into a bustling industrial town. This demographic shift brought with it a host of challenges, including the need for housing, sanitation, and social infrastructure. The town's landscape was dotted with workers' cottages, factory buildings, and other structures reflecting the changing needs of a rapidly industrializing society.

One of the key drivers of Bonnybridge's industrial success was the harnessing of water power. Mills and factories along the Bonny Water river utilized water wheels to generate mechanical power, revolutionizing the production processes. This innovation not only increased efficiency but also laid the groundwork for the subsequent adoption of steam power. The rhythmic churning of water wheels became synonymous with Bonnybridge's industrial identity, symbolizing the town's ability to harness natural resources for economic gain.

The availability of coal in the Bonnybridge region played a pivotal role in sustaining the town's industrial activities. Coal mining became a significant industry, providing a constant supply of fuel to power the steam engines driving the machinery in the factories. The mines employed a substantial portion of the local population, creating a symbiotic relationship between the mining and manufacturing sectors. The blackened landscape, scarred by coal pits and industrial structures, stood as a testament to the town's reliance on this essential resource.

Iron ore, another abundant resource in the vicinity, further galvanised Bonnybridge's industrial expansion. The iron industry in Bonnybridge flourished, producing a wide range of goods, including tools, machinery, and construction materials. The integration of iron production with other industries catalysed a broader economic transformation, turning Bonnybridge into a multifaceted industrial centre.

The strategic location of Bonnybridge along the Forth and Clyde Canal was a key factor in its economic success. The canal provided a cost-effective and efficient means of transporting raw materials and finished products, connecting Bonnybridge to the major industrial centres of Glasgow and Edinburgh. This connectivity not only facilitated the inflow of essential resources but also enabled the outflow of Bonnybridge's products to wider markets, contributing to the town's economic growth.

The Forth and Clyde Canal, with its intricate network of locks and basins, played a crucial role in shaping Bonnybridge's industrial landscape. Warehouses lined the canal banks, serving as storage facilities for raw materials and finished goods. The canal also hosted a bustling scene of cargo boats, transporting coal, iron, textiles, and other commodities to and from Bonnybridge. The waterway became a conduit for economic exchange, linking Bonnybridge to the broader economic landscape of 18th-century Britain.

The impact of the Industrial Revolution on Bonnybridge extended beyond the economic sphere, influencing social and cultural aspects of the community. The rapid urbanization and industrialization brought about a shift in lifestyle, as traditional agrarian practices gave way to factory work. The once-close-knit rural community experienced a transformation, with a diverse influx of workers from different regions converging in Bonnybridge to seek employment in the burgeoning industries.

The changing demographic makeup of Bonnybridge necessitated the development of social infrastructure. Housing for the growing population became a priority, leading to the construction of workers' cottages and tenement buildings. The architecture of Bonnybridge evolved to accommodate the needs of an industrial society, with utilitarian structures dominating the landscape.

The rise of industrial capitalism in Bonnybridge also brought about changes in labour relations. The factory system introduced a structured work environment, with fixed working hours and wages. Labour unions emerged as workers sought to advocate for better working conditions and fair wages. Strikes and labour disputes became part of Bonnybridge's industrial narrative, reflecting the tensions inherent in the transition from agrarian to industrial society.

Despite the challenges, the Industrial Revolution brought unprecedented economic prosperity to Bonnybridge. The town's industries thrived, contributing to the overall economic growth of the region. Bonnybridge became known for its iron products, textiles, and other manufactured goods, gaining recognition as a significant industrial centre in Scotland.

As the 19th century unfolded, technological advancements continued to shape Bonnybridge's industrial landscape. The transition from water power to steam power marked a new phase in industrialization. Steam engines replaced water wheels, offering a more reliable and versatile source of power. The distinctive sound of steam engines became the new soundtrack of Bonnybridge, echoing through the industrial precincts.

The advent of the railway further enhanced Bonnybridge's connectivity. The town became a railway junction, linking it to the expanding rail network across Scotland. The railway facilitated the transportation of goods to distant markets and accelerated the movement of people, fostering greater mobility and exchange.

The continued growth of industry in Bonnybridge, however, was not without its challenges. Environmental degradation became a pressing concern as industrial activities led to pollution of air and water. The once pristine Bonny Water river now bore the brunt of industrial effluents, impacting the ecosystem and raising environmental awareness among the residents.

By the late 19th century, Bonnybridge, like many other industrial towns, faced the complexities of a mature industrial society. Economic fluctuations, technological shifts, and social tensions posed challenges to the sustainability of the town's industrial base. The optimism that characterized the early days of industrialization gave way to a more nuanced understanding of the benefits and pitfalls of rapid industrial growth.

The 20th century witnessed further transformations in Bonnybridge's industrial landscape. The decline of traditional industries, coupled with changes in global economic dynamics, led to the diversification of the town's economic base. New industries emerged, reflecting the shift towards a service-oriented economy. The once-dominant industrial sector made room for technological advancements, education, and healthcare.

The closing decades of the 20th century saw efforts to preserve Bonnybridge's industrial heritage. Historical societies, preservationists, and local authorities collaborated to safeguard key industrial sites and structures. The remnants of water wheels, canal infrastructure, and factory buildings became historical landmarks, serving as a tangible link to Bonnybridge's industrial past.

Bonnybridge's journey during the Industrial Revolution exemplifies the transformative power of industrialization on a community's landscape and economic dynamics. The convergence of natural resources, technological innovation, and strategic geographical positioning positioned Bonnybridge as a key contributor to Britain's industrial prowess, leaving an indelible mark on its history and shaping its identity for generations to come. The legacy of Bonnybridge's industrial past continues to echo through its present, reminding us of the profound impact of the Industrial Revolution on the evolution of communities and societies.

However, during the latter part of the 20th century UFO reports from eye-witnesses and experiencers began to gain momentum.

CHAPTER FOUR

The Birth of Bonnybridge UFO Sightings

The First Reports

The first documented reports of unusual sightings in Bonnybridge, a small town in Scotland, emerged in the early 1990s, marking the beginning of a mysterious and ongoing phenomenon. Residents in the area began reporting sightings of strange lights and unidentified flying objects in the sky, sparking curiosity and concern among the local community.

What set these accounts apart was not just the isolated nature of the sightings, but rather the consistent and recurrent nature of the events. Witnesses claimed to have observed inexplicable phenomena over an extended period, with reports ranging from peculiar lights hovering in the night sky to unidentified objects exhibiting unconventional flight patterns. The sheer frequency of these incidents prompted both local authorities and researchers to pay attention to the phenomenon unfolding in Bonnybridge.

As reports continued to accumulate, the town gained a reputation as a hotspot for UFO activity. Researchers and investigators delved into the phenomenon, seeking explanations for the unusual occurrences. Various theories emerged, ranging from the conventional, such as misidentified aircraft or natural atmospheric phenomena, to the more speculative, involving extra-terrestrial visitations.

Local authorities, initially sceptical, eventually found themselves grappling with the growing number of eyewitness accounts. Concerns about public safety and a desire to address the community's growing unease led to official investigations. Government agencies, including law enforcement and aviation authorities, joined forces with researchers and UFO enthusiasts to scrutinize the phenomena occurring in Bonnybridge.

Despite concerted efforts to uncover the truth, the mystery of Bonnybridge persisted, with sightings continuing to baffle both residents and investigators alike. The town became a focal point for those interested in the unexplained, drawing attention from media outlets and sparking debates within the scientific and paranormal communities.

Over the years, Bonnybridge's reputation as a UFO hotspot has endured, and the phenomenon remains an intriguing and unsolved mystery. The ongoing reports of unusual sightings have left an indelible mark on the town, shaping its identity and making it a unique case study in the realm of unidentified aerial phenomena. The events in Bonnybridge serve as a reminder that, even in the modern age, there are still mysteries that elude explanation and continue to capture the imagination of those who seek to unravel the secrets of the cosmos.

Eyewitness Accounts

Eyewitness accounts, crucial components of the reports, painted a vivid tapestry of unusual phenomena that captivated the imagination of the local population. Residents shared narratives filled with intrigue, describing encounters with enigmatic lights, bewildering movements, and unconventional shapes that defied the familiar contours of known aircraft. The collective testimony created a compelling mosaic, fostering a sense of shared curiosity and concern within the community.

The descriptions provided by the eyewitnesses went beyond mere sightings; they delved into the realm of the extraordinary. Witnesses often spoke of lights that danced across the night sky, their luminosity fluctuating in a manner inconsistent with conventional aircraft. Some reported abrupt changes in direction and speed, manoeuvres that surpassed the capabilities of any known technology. These anomalous movements left onlookers both awe-inspired and perplexed, fuelling speculation about the nature and origin of these mysterious objects.

The shapes described in these accounts were equally perplexing. Witnesses struggled to relate the forms they observed to any conventional aircraft or celestial bodies. Unconventional silhouettes, geometric configurations, and unorthodox aerial patterns were frequently mentioned. These reports transcended the mundane, suggesting that whatever soared overhead possessed characteristics beyond the scope of conventional understanding.

What added weight to these accounts was the striking consistency among the witnesses? Residents from various locations independently reported similar details, reinforcing the credibility of the sightings. The resonance of these shared experiences not only heightened the sense of wonder but also instilled a sense of unease among some residents, prompting a collective desire for answers.

As the eyewitness narratives circulated, they ignited a broader discourse within the community. Local media outlets featured stories of these encounters, fostering a communal dialogue about the unexplained phenomena. Residents gathered in forums and town hall meetings to share their experiences, exchange theories, and collectively grapple with the mysterious events unfolding above.

In essence, the eyewitness accounts became a catalyst for a deeper exploration into the unknown, propelling the community into a shared journey of discovery and contemplation. The strange lights, unconventional movements, and mysterious shapes in the sky had not only captivated individual imaginations but had also woven a tapestry of intrigue that bound the community together in a quest for understanding. Many of these eye witness statements will be explored further in this chapter.

Billy Buchanan, long-standing local Councillor and UFO investigator, claimed that in 1992 a local man had a horrific encounter with a UFO that announced Bonnybridge to the world of the weird and strange. Buchanan claimed on the Real Britannia TV show that Mr James Walker had a close encounter with lights and a UFO. He was driving down a back road from Falkirk when "a strange situation and lights" occurred ahead of him. Walker apparently confided in Buchanan the next day and Buchanan announced it to the local press the following day to see if anyone else had witnessed the UFO. Buchanan states that he couldn't believe just how many people came forward to tell him about their UFO experience.

But finally, I want to return to my childhood in the 1960s. This is when my curiosity about the UFO phenomenon began. My grandmother, Isabella Anderson, would tell me about the "wee folk" she had seen in the 1920s on the Falkirk to Bonnybridge road. She recounted that a large saucer-shaped object moved silently above a woodland towards her and her mother in broad daylight. It was early morning in the summertime, and they were delivering milk to the locals on a pony and trap. The sight petrified them both. Not to mention the pony that bolted up the lane.

She said that the saucer hovered close to them, about twenty feet above their heads. She began to scream and fell to the ground at the sight of the "wee folk" peering out of the small, round windows in the craft. Seconds later, the saucer vanished, and they were left chasing the pony and trap down the lane.

Craig Malcolm

In 2002, the BBC published an article about one experiencer's claims. Scottish farm worker Craig Malcolm tells of his years scanning the skies for unidentified flying objects.

"My nephew, who is four, loves watching the skies. We did the ET ride at Universal Studios and the wee man thought it was brilliant. Now he thinks ET is going to come and see him.

"I saw my first UFO in 1991 when I was 19. My big brother came into the house one night pure white - we thought he'd been in a car crash. He said, 'something's just chased me' - yeah, right. We went outside and this thing was above our house. The only way I can describe it is a figure of eight rotating through the sky.

"There was no sound; just pulsating lights coming off it. We videoed it, and when we played it back, we noticed smaller objects coming off it and flying off in opposite directions.

"From there, it just snowballed. I've seen about 180 now, and have got 13 hours of footage of strange phenomena flying about in the sky above my house. I've also filmed planes and helicopters just to compare them.

"I sent this footage to SETI [the Search for Extra-terrestrial Intelligence Institute] in the US for analysis. It came back that 95% was UFOs and 5% was aircraft. I'd been a bit of a sceptic before I saw what I saw; I'm a 100% believer now.

"I've had a few hair-raising experiences. Something chased me while I was in the car with my dad. We believe there's something strange here, whether it be government or UFO

"We'd seen something hovering and had got out to have a look when two balls came out as if to get us. At that point I jumped back in the car - I was all for leaving my dad on the side of the road, I was that terrified.

"As we drove off, we noticed a red BMW sitting in a lay-by so stopped to ask if they'd seen it. These two guys said that they hadn't seen anything and that they didn't want to talk to us. Then they just drove off.

"The next day, the police came to my work - I'd been in a company vehicle the night before - and asked why I'd been on that road. By the end of the week, I'd lost my job. There's a hell of a lot of activity, with military helicopters and such like flying about.

"I know it's typical to blame the government, but I worked for the Ministry of Defence a while back and had my eyes opened by that job. I drove senior staff to and from military establishments all over the place - there's a lot more out there than people like to believe.

"People who haven't seen things tend to be total sceptics and call me a crackpot. But I'm a pretty level-headed sort of guy and I don't drink or take drugs. I know what I've seen, what my family's seen. These things are totally bizarre. They do neck-breaking manoeuvres. They disappear and reappear in different places. We've seen discs, triangles, tubes, spheres, all different lights and colours. We all believe there's something strange, whether it be government or UFO. I reckon we'll never really find out what's out there."

Andrew Hennessey

Author of *The Mystery of Stargate Edinburgh*, Andrew Hennessey, said: "I believe that the United Kingdom is one of the most underground places on the planet; particularly central Scotland. Central Scotland has got the most untalked about cavern systems on the planet."

How does he come to this remarkable conclusion? Hennessey noticed that across Scotland there were a large number of pylons, secret sites and fenced off areas. To anyone else, then, it has been regular NATO bases. But for Hennessey they were simply superficial signs of all that covert activity under the ground.

"It stretches all the way up into Dunfermline for miles and miles and miles. Over the transmitters and pylons and dishes of the military command centre itself."

Hennessey claims that he saw a glowing cuboid spaceship. With lots of blue lights. Furthermore, he states that near Bonnybridge, he has discovered an entrance to one of the tunnels.

"This is a fire exit on the southern approaches to one of the biggest command centres, probably in Western Europe. It's a fire exit for the underground base."

But if you're wondering what the aliens and the military are up to in the underground bases, then Hennessey explains: "Extra-terrestrials live in a Galaxy-wide empire and the Earth is merely the marketplace. A huge empire operating a portal system, and I think some of that portal system is in Bonnybridge."

According to Hennessay, aliens don't fly through space in the conventional sense. Instead, they use gateways between their Galaxy and ours, and they can be found in important locations all over the planet.

"Some say that they time travel, how they go through interdimensional portals, that they come back and forth here."

If Hennessey's theory is correct it might explain why UFO's congregated in hotspots. If there is an alien gateway in Scotland, where is it? Let's run with the idea for a moment. First, let's take that map of the Falkirk triangle. I've plotted all the sightings over the last 30 years. At first, they seem random, scattered over 500 square miles, and some do appear to be near military bases.

40 miles from Bonnybridge, there's another place where UFO

sightings seem to congregate. It's a small town called Rosslyn. In the southern corner of the Falkirk triangle. It's from here that some of the most detailed accounts have come, and one of the clearest photographs of what's said to be a UFO. On the Andrew Hennessy was used as evidence that spaceship was photographed on the same night in the vicinity of Rosslyn.

Rosslyn Town is unremarkable at first glance. But there is one place in the town that is remarkable: Rosslyn Chapel. This just happens to be one of the most mysterious places in the whole of the world. As far back as 700BC there is strong evidence of the Druids being here.

It's also been the focus of some of the weirdest conspiracy theories going. So here's what we know for sure. Rosslyn Chapel was built in 1446 by William St. Clair. He was rumoured to be one of the Christians called the Knights Templar. They were very rich and powerful. Until the Pope excommunicated them. It's since been claimed that the Templars had found the secret of eternal life.

Now the mystery of Rosslyn has been added to by a series of bizarre UFO sightings. Scottish ufologists, Ron Halliday, has documented most of them.

"There have been UFO sightings in the area over the years," said Halliday. "Triangular shaped objects, disc shaped objects, objects hovering in the sky, objects on the ground, and of course, in addition, people have claimed to have seen non-human entities."

Some people have since suggested that extra-terrestrials might have been responsible for certain inexplicable things inside the chapel. The carvings of American Maze apparently edged into the walls before America was discovered. And the vines that wrapped themselves around The Apprentice pillar. A seemingly perfect representation of the double Helix of DNA. Did ETs give William St. Clair the knowledge from the future to leave these messages? Outrageous idea. But maybe not outrageous enough. For some levels are convinced that something even more potent, because the Holy Grail is buried at the Chapel. The gateway to another dimension used by aliens. But where did they get this idea? Well, from almost the first time people began to see UFOs, they said they saw them most around buildings with rich histories and mystical pasts. Structures like the pyramids of Egypt. Stonehenge in England. Now add to that Scotland's Rosslyn Chapel. According to some, all these ancient sites are gateways to other parallel dimensions. And this would explain why sightings are concentrated around these sacred places.

Hennessey says: "I think that that that these sites have been used for traveling between dimensions and worlds."

Media Attention

As reports of UAP sightings in Bonnybridge gained momentum, the media quickly caught wind of the story. Newspapers, television channels, and radio stations flocked to the town to cover the mysterious events unfolding in its skies. The increased media attention brought both fascination and scepticism, with experts and enthusiasts debating the nature of the phenomena witnessed by Bonnybridge residents.

In 2010, the BBC claimed that reports of "flying Toblerones" and objects travelling at 1,100 mph across the Scottish sky were released by the Ministry of Defence. The files detailed how unidentified objects have been witnessed flying over a range of locations across Scotland.

Among them were one from a senior air traffic controller at Prestwick Airport who reported seeing a fast-moving UFO on the airport radar.

While four fishermen spotted a flat, shiny object hovering off the coast. The Scottish accounts are among the thousands of reports made of close encounters with UFOs across the UK which have been released in a joint project between the MoD and the National Archives.

The Prestwick airport incident in February 1999 led to an extensive investigation by RAF air defence staff who impounded radar tapes from a number of airports around the UK. But the report concluded that no additional evidence could be found to corroborate what the air traffic controller had spotted.

In another file, a report reveals four members of the crew of a fishing trawler in the North Sea spotted a flat, shiny, round object hovering 19 miles north-east of Fraserburgh on 18 August 1997. They tracked the mysterious UFO on their surface radar for several seconds before it vanished.

Also included in the previously top secret files is the testimony of a West Lothian electrician who spotted a "Toblerone-shaped" UFO hovering over a field. A sketch of the craft is included in the report.

Other document describe a request submitted to former Prime Minister Tony Blair from a councillor for an inquiry into 600 alleged sightings in the so-called Bonnybridge Triangle, near Falkirk. The files contain verbal and drawn accounts of UFO encounters

The area is renowned among enthusiasts as being among the best places in the world to see UFOs. In October 1997, Bonnybridge councillor Billy Buchanan, of Falkirk District Council, wrote to Mr Blair demanding the phenomena were investigated after five years of pursuing the matter.

He wrote: "For five years the people both you and I represent have witnessed a phenomenon in the area that has been left unexplained.

"I wrote to your predecessor John Major, I have also contacted our local MP Dennis Canavan who put me in contact with the MoD who told me quite strongly that nothing was happening in Bonnybridge that was a threat to national security."

He continued: "I have tried to get an answer for the people and have been ridiculed for it." I appeal to you Mr Blair to get the phenomenon investigated."

A MoD response to the letter said there were no grounds to investigate the matter. But Mr Buchanan did not give up and wrote to Mr Blair once again in 1998 demanding "the truth".

Experts believe the records highlight how shapes of reported UFOs have changed over the last few decades, possibly explained by representations of UFOs in popular culture. Many reports in this latest file describe aircraft as big, black and triangular in shape with lights along the edges, whereas the predominant form in the 1940s to 1950s was saucer or disc-shaped.

Stuart Campbell, the Edinburgh-based author of the book The UFO Mystery Solved, said: "UFO reports have all sorts of explanations - lights in the sky from aircraft to hot air balloons. "Every mystery has a solution somewhere, everything has a rational explanation. The alternative is that we don't live in a rational universe. "The job is to find an explanation and that can be hard work sometimes."

In 2023, The Herald, Scotland, wrote in an article, that in general terms, Falkirk and Bermuda have little in common. Yet they share the honorific "Triangle".

This Triangle indicates a place where mysterious happenings occur – in The Bermuda Triangle disappearances, in The Falkirk Triangle appearances of UFOs.

Our area of investigation is also known as The Bonnybridge Triangle, as the large village of that name is the centre of the weirdness. And we mean world centre, the "UFO capital of the world."

The biggest mystery surrounding the phenomenon is: why Bonnybridge? It has no Pentagon or Kremlin. Bonnybridge may be found in the west of the Falkirk council area in the central belt. The Bonny Water flows through it, the Forth and Clyde Canal sits just south of it. The village population is just under 7,000. However, the "settlement area", including Banknock, Denny, Dunipace and Haggs has around 25,000. The area's industrial history featured mills, brickworks and iron foundries.

Bonnybridge's association with UFOs began in 1992 when businessman James Walker, driving home on the Falkirk-Bonnyrigg road, was forced to stop his car after a cross-shaped formation of brightly shining objects hovered above the road ahead. This then changed shape to a triangle before legging it quickly back to the cosmos. James did similar, back to Bonnybridge.

After that, UFO sightings in the area came in thick and fast. In his level-headed book UFO Scotland, investigator Ron Halliday details some of these. In March 1992, for example, the Slogett family were walking towards Bonnybridge one evening when they saw a circle of blue light in the sky. Then a craft "the size of a house" landing in nearby moorland.

Isabella Slogett recalled: "A door opened and there was a howl-like sound." The Slogetts legged it, pursued by two small craft, but luckily made it back home safely. After this, understandably, mild hysteria took hold, with actual ufologists urging people to calm down.

In December 1992, a television "skywatch" over the area was broadcast, but nothing appeared. Still, sightings continued. In May 1996, 63-year-old Margaret Ross of Stenhousemuir recorded video footage of an ultra-bright, disc-shaped light criss-crossed by different colours.

In 1997, father and son Jim and Craig Malcolm, of Larbert, filmed a "spinning orb", followed shortly afterwards by a military jet. There is more about Craig Malcolm's multiple UFO encounters later in this book.

Many residents went to local councillor Billy Buchanan. He took up their case, writing to the late Queen and the Ministry of Defence, demanding an investigation. Backed by noted ufologists Malcolm

Robinson, he also appealed to a succession of prime ministers, each of whom gave him the rubber ear.

According to Mr Buchanan, almost half the town's residents have seen a UFO and, every year, about 300 reports are received. In the area encompassing Stirling, Cumbernauld and Falkirk, more than 60,000 people out of a population of 165,000 have supposedly reported sightings.

Mr Buchanan, below, a popular figure and man of the people, whom he's served faithfully for 25 years, says he still receives regular reports. "Probably every week there's somebody'll phone me up and say that they've saw something that they can't explain."

Obviously this led to tense situations. Ufologists arrived "but nobody ever came and actually gave us a defined answer".

He said the latest theories involved time travel and a UFO base in the sea. While retaining an open mind, he claimed governments concealed the truth. "I wouldn't believe one word that came out of any politician's mouth," said the councillor.

Other theories purporting to explain the phenomenon include that, like its counterpart in Bermuda, the Falkirk Triangle is a window into another dimension.

Or the objects could be secret military craft, while sceptics also point to the fact that the village lies beneath various flight paths. This wouldn't account for the close, personal encounters, though some of these have been explained.

The aforementioned Mr Halliday instances the case of a supposed UFO sighting that turned out to be lights from a jeep club's bumpy racing competition nearby.

Some cynics say "Scotland's Roswell" – after the famous New Mexico site of an alleged saucer crash in 1947 – is, or has become, a bogus scheme concocted to encourage business and tourism.

It may have kosher origins but the councillor has made the most of it to win publicity for the area. Well, who could blame him?

But, while mass hysteria and confirmation bias might be adduced, it's difficult to imagine so many ordinary citizens taking part in a promo scam. What are they getting out of it? A rates reduction?

As in The X Files, we "want to believe", of course. But it's difficult with impressive video evidence still mysteriously lacking, even today when you can hardly take a wizz up an alley without someone capturing it on film (no, madam, I'm not speaking from experience).

Billy Buchanan

Billy Buchanan, a resident of Bonnybridge, Scotland, has become a local legend known for his avid interest in UFOs and extra-terrestrial phenomena. Born and raised in this small town nestled amidst the picturesque landscapes, Billy's fascination with the skies above began at a young age.

Growing up in the shadow of the Falkirk Triangle, an area known for its higher-than-average number of reported UFO sightings, Billy found himself captivated by the mysterious happenings in the heavens. His childhood curiosity evolved into a lifelong passion, leading him to immerse himself in the study of unidentified flying objects and related mysteries.

Billy became an active member of various UFO enthusiast communities, attending conferences and connecting with like-minded individuals who shared his fascination. He started documenting local sightings, interviewing witnesses, and collecting data on unexplained phenomena in and around Bonnybridge. His meticulous record-keeping and attention to detail earned him a reputation as the go-to person for anything related to UFOs in the region.

In the heart of Bonnybridge, Billy established a small UFO research centre, a quaint space filled with books, maps, and charts detailing reported sightings. Local residents, intrigued by the mysteries that seemed to swirl above their town, often visited to share their own experiences or seek Billy's insights. His willingness to listen and genuine enthusiasm for the subject endeared him to the community.

Billy's efforts extended beyond simply cataloguing sightings. He organized night sky observation events, inviting residents to join him in scanning the heavens for any unusual activity. These gatherings fostered a sense of camaraderie among locals and further fuelled the town's reputation as a hub for UFO enthusiasts.

Over the years, Billy Buchanan became a recognizable figure in Bonnybridge, often featured in local news stories and documentaries about the area's UFO phenomena. His knowledge, combined with his amiable personality, made him a respected voice in the UFO community.

While sceptics might dismiss the sightings as mere coincidences or natural phenomena, Billy's unwavering dedication to exploring the unknown has left an indelible mark on Bonnybridge. Whether believers or sceptics, residents can't deny the impact of Billy Buchanan's UFO interests on the town's identity, making him a unique and cherished character in the local tapestry of mysteries and wonders.

Billy Buchanan's influence extended beyond the confines of Bonnybridge, reaching a global audience through his active involvement in UFO research and advocacy. His commitment to unravelling the mysteries of the skies drew attention from the wider UFO community, turning him into a respected figure in the field.

In addition to local gatherings, Billy began participating in national and international UFO conferences, where he shared his insights and findings. His presentations, often peppered with anecdotes from Bonnybridge, captivated audiences, sparking discussions about the nature of extra-terrestrial encounters and the potential implications for humanity.

Billy's research wasn't limited to collecting eyewitness accounts. He delved into the historical records, studying centuries-old reports of unusual phenomena in the area. His investigations aimed to establish patterns and correlations, adding a historical context to the contemporary UFO sightings around Bonnybridge.

His dedication to scientific rigor also led him to collaborate with researchers and experts in related fields. He engaged with astronomers, physicists, and psychologists to explore various angles of the phenomenon. This interdisciplinary approach added depth to his work, elevating the discourse around UFOs beyond mere speculation.

Despite encountering scepticism, Billy maintained an open-minded and diplomatic approach, fostering a healthy dialogue between believers and sceptics. He emphasized the importance of critical thinking and empirical evidence while encouraging an exploration of the unknown. This inclusive attitude contributed to the credibility of his work and endeared him to a broad spectrum of individuals interested in the extra-terrestrial unknown.

Beyond his research, Billy sought to educate the public about UFO phenomena. He authored articles, contributed to documentaries, and even hosted a local radio show, sharing his knowledge and inviting experts to discuss the latest developments in the field. This outreach effort aimed to demystify the subject, empowering individuals to engage with the topic in an informed manner.

As Billy's influence grew, so did the recognition of Bonnybridge as a significant location in the study of UFOs. The town became a destination for enthusiasts and researchers alike, drawn by the allure of the Falkirk Triangle and the compelling stories curated by Billy Buchanan.

But while Billy Buchanan has written time after time to successive government ministers and Prime Ministers, his attempts to get them to take the issue seriously have been in vain. Billy's legacy endured, and his contributions to the exploration of UFO phenomena left an indelible mark on the town of Bonnybridge. Whether inspiring the next generation of researchers or continuing to fuel public interest in the mysteries of the cosmos, Billy Buchanan became a central figure in the ongoing quest to understand the unexplained.

Investigations and Research

The Bonnybridge sightings prompted various independent investigations and research initiatives. UFO enthusiasts, paranormal investigators, and academics delved into the phenomenon, attempting to uncover the truth behind the mysterious occurrences. Some researchers conducted interviews with eyewitnesses, while others analysed photographs and videos captured during the sightings.

Malcolm Robinson has been a prominent figure in the field of ufology, particularly in the context of Bonnybridge and the reported UFO sightings in the area. His involvement extends beyond just being a witness; he has dedicated a significant portion of his career to researching, documenting, and advocating for a serious investigation into the phenomenon.

Robinson is known for his meticulous approach to UFO investigations. He has interviewed numerous witnesses who claimed to have experienced sightings in and around Bonnybridge, gathering detailed accounts to better understand the nature of the reported phenomena. His work often involves scrutinizing photographic and video evidence, attempting to discern patterns or commonalities among the sightings.

Beyond his direct involvement with witnesses, Robinson has also engaged with the wider public, raising awareness about the Bonnybridge UFO sightings and advocating for a more scientific and open-minded approach to the study of unidentified flying objects. He has written articles, given interviews, and participated in conferences to share his findings and perspectives on the subject.

While the concept of UFOs often carries a degree of scepticism, Robinson has sought to approach the phenomenon with a balanced and rational mind-set. His work contributes to the ongoing dialogue about the nature of UFO sightings, encouraging a serious examination of the data and experiences reported by individuals in the Bonnybridge Triangle.

Indeed, in 2023, Robinson appealed to Britain's Prime Minister in an a televised Talk TV interview saying, "Rishi Sunak, we have got to open up a government enquiry, because we have the evidence that something strange is amiss in the skies above Central Scotland."

Malcolm Robinson's connection to Bonnybridge UFOs goes beyond being a witness; he is a dedicated ufologists and investigator who has played a crucial role in collecting and analysing data related to the reported sightings in the region, contributing significantly to the understanding of the Bonnybridge Triangle phenomenon.

Community Impact

The impact of the UAP sightings on the Bonnybridge community was multifaceted. While some residents embraced the newfound attention, others were wary of the potential consequences, fearing that the town's reputation could be tarnished. The sightings also brought together individuals who shared similar experiences, fostering a sense of community among those who believed they had witnessed something extraordinary.

Primetime TV presenter, Michael Aspel, highlighted the Bonnybridge/Falkirk phenomenon in a TV special in 1994 called *Strange But True* S1. E3. Filmed at Falkirk Town Hall, experiencers recounted the impact their encounters with UFOs. In a packed hall, they wanted answers.

"In the past few years, nowhere has had more UFO reports than a certain part of Scotland," said Aspel in his introduction to the TV episode. "In the skies around the town of Falkirk in the last couple of years, around 800 UFOs have been sighted. It's a phenomena of such proportions that anxious locals have called a public meeting. They want to know the truth: what's behind the sudden upsurge?"

Witnesses at the meeting stated a variety of UFO phenomena, from low clouds with revolving lights inside, to objects that flared up and dulled down again. One experiencers said it was "as if a light was turning towards me and turning away again."

Another experiencer said, "Suddenly it started to move away, not very quickly, then suddenly collapsed in on itself and disappeared."

Aspel says that Ray and Kathy Prosek were driving along a motorway nearby Bonnybridge. As they approached a via-duct, spanning the road, they say they saw an object the size of a jumbo jet, hovering above it.

"I could see it was triangular in shape, with a light on each corner," claimed Ray Prosek. "We passed underneath the via-duct, and looking back, there sitting on the other side was another craft. And it looked like a mirror image, the way they were pointing towards each other."

"It didn't look like anything I'd ever seen before," said Kathy Prosek. "So of course you automatically think: UFO."

Driving home to the neighbouring Larbert, Neil Malcolm, says he was followed home by a ball of light.

"I got the fright of my life really," said Neil Malcolm. "I knew it wasn't anybody's headlights, or anything, because it lit up the full interior of the car."

He rushed in to tell the rest of the family. Neil's wife, Lorraine, grabbed her video camera.

"I zoomed in," said Lorraine Malcom. "I wasn't sure what I could see. You know what a plane or a helicopter looks like, it definitely wasn't anything like that."

The footage shows a large ball of light moving in a zig-zag motion just above the roof tops. It then disappears out of sight behind the houses. Expert analysis of the footage have been unable to reveal what it might be.

UFO researcher, Malcolm Robinson, stated that he checked with airports and he also checked with local police and with metrological stations to see if there were any weather balloons. He did this routinely, because as a serious UFO research, he stated that 95% of all sightings were mis-identifications. But he stated there was "a small residue which was highly unusual, and demanded further investigation."

Ongoing Phenomena

The UAP sightings in Bonnybridge did not cease after the initial reports; instead, they persisted over the years. The town became a focal point for those interested in UFO phenomena, drawing visitors and researchers eager to witness or study the unexplained events. This ongoing interest turned Bonnybridge into a unique case study within the broader field of ufology.

Bonnybridge's association with unidentified aerial phenomena has left an indelible mark on the town's history. The first reports of strange occurrences in the skies catapulted this Scottish community into the global spotlight, sparking debates, investigations, and ongoing interest in the unexplained. Whether one is a sceptic, a believer, or a curious onlooker, the enigma of Bonnybridge continues to captivate the imagination and challenge our understanding of the mysteries that unfold above us.

CHAPTER FIVE

The Falkirk Triangle & Other Worldwide UFO Hot Spots

As we delve into the unknown realms of unidentified flying objects, our journey takes us to diverse corners of the globe, each shrouded in its unique mystique. In this chapter, we embark on a comparative exploration of the Falkirk Triangle in Bonnybridge and other UFO hotspots worldwide, seeking patterns, anomalies, and shared narratives that transcend geographical boundaries.

Nestled within the scenic landscapes of Scotland, the Falkirk Triangle has gained notoriety for being a hotbed of UFO sightings, mysterious lights, and unexplained phenomena. Local residents speak in hushed tones about encounters that defy conventional explanation. From luminous orbs hovering silently in the night sky to bizarre geometric formations witnessed by startled onlookers, the Falkirk Triangle remains an enigma that beckons researchers and enthusiasts alike.

In 1994, Michael Aspel stated that the most puzzling UFO incident happened in woodlands near Livingston, a few miles from Bonnybridge. It was a case that police came to officially investigate as assault by person or persons unknown. It happened to a forestry work, Bob Taylor, who was out on patrol checking for stray sheep in the forest.

As he rounded a corner, he discovered something else. "It was a huge thing, with a big round dome. A very dark grey colour. It had a big flange going all the way around it. I could see arms sticking out of this flange, with what I took to be blades on top. Two balls came out. I think they'd be about 3 feet in diameter, with about 6 spikes. They came right up beside me. I remember feeling a tug at that time."

Bob Taylor couldn't remember what happened next.

The next thing he did remember was lying on the ground dazed and bleeding. Unable to walk and in no condition to drive, he set off for help on his hands and knees. By the time he arrived home, he was in a state of near total collapse.

Bob's wife stated that he looked shocked and was drained – quiet white. His face was dirty. She thought he'd had a crash in his vehicle. But Bob said that he'd been attacked.

"I said what with? And he said, a spaceship! I said oh goodness me, there's no such thing as a spaceship. I'm going to phone the doctor. You must have fell and hurt your head."

Bob's wife called Bob's boss, Malcom Drummond. He went to the forest and found Bob's abandoned truck. And that was all. In the clearing he found impressions had been made in the ground.

"There is no doubt in my mind," Malcolm Drummond said, "that these marks were made by a perfectly solid heavier than air object. They had been made by some machine that had come vertically down. There's no doubt about that."

The area was fenced off and police began an intensive search. They found nothing. It was one of the most puzzling cases that Detective Inspector, Ian Wark, ever worked on.

"I couldn't believe at first," Wark said. "The ground was soft. And there was no sign of the tracks having come from somewhere, or having went anywhere. They just seemed to have arrived."

Near the caterpillar-type tracks were holes in the ground – 3 inches deep. 40 holes in all.

"At first I thought they had possibly been made by equipment used by the forestry commission," said Wark. "But we went to their premises later that day and examined all the vehicles, and nothing at all matched."

Taylor's trousers had also been ripped. He claimed that they had been made by the UFO. The trousers were sent by the police to forensic expert, Lester Nibb, who stated: "There were two sets of damage predominantly. Close enough to be considered symmetrical. It's obviously been cause by a lifting action. It's not the kind of action caused by a fall, a tear would normally be down the trousers. Certainly the story could fit the bill. Some object or objects had moved across the clearing towards him, attempted to lift him up and carry him off."

Detective Inspector Wark concluded that "even to this day we are completely baffled. One: who assaulted Mr Taylor? And two, what made these marks on the ground?"

Bob Taylor, who died in 2007, was a respected war hero and teetotal churchgoer. No-one doubted that he was sincere in what he believed he had seen and throughout the rest of his life he never deviated from his story.

The Ariel School UFO Incident

The Ariel School UFO incident, which occurred on September 16, 1994, in Ruwa, Zimbabwe, is a fascinating and well-documented case in the realm of UFO encounters. Over sixty students at the Ariel School reported witnessing a peculiar event where a silver craft landed in a field near their school. The students described seeing beings dressed in all black who exited the mysterious silver object.

This incident gained significant attention due to the sheer number of witnesses, particularly children, and the consistency in their descriptions of the event. The encounter unfolded during a morning break, and the students claimed to have seen the silver craft descend and land in a nearby field. The beings that emerged were described as wearing all-black attire.

What makes this case particularly compelling is the sincerity and consistency of the testimonies provided by the young witnesses. The students independently recounted similar details, describing the beings as having large eyes and being able to communicate with them telepathically. Some even claimed to have received messages about the Earth's ecological state and the need for environmental preservation.

The incident was investigated by various researchers and experts in the field of ufology, adding an element of credibility to the accounts. Psychologists and investigators interviewed the students to assess the authenticity of their experiences. The consistency in their stories, despite the children not having any prior knowledge of UFO encounters, added weight to the overall credibility of the incident.

Let's have a look at some of the compelling facts.

Witness Accounts: The students' descriptions of the beings were consistent, with details such as large, black eyes, smooth skin, and communication through telepathy. Some students reported feeling a sense of communication or a message being conveyed to them, emphasizing the importance of environmental conservation.

Number of Witnesses: Over sixty students, ranging in age from 5 to 12, claimed to have witnessed the event. The large number of witnesses, all from the same location and time, adds credibility to the incident.

Interviews and Investigation: Researchers and investigators, including prominent ufologist Cynthia Hind, visited the school to conduct interviews and gather information. The children were interviewed separately, and their stories were found to be remarkably consistent, supporting the authenticity of their accounts.

Effects on Witnesses: Some students reported experiencing

psychological and emotional effects after the incident, including vivid dreams and a heightened sense of awareness. The encounter left a lasting impact on many of the witnesses, shaping their perspectives on life and the existence of extra-terrestrial beings.

Media Coverage: The incident received widespread media coverage, both locally and internationally. It became one of the well-documented and publicized UFO encounters involving multiple witnesses.

Sketches and Drawings: Many of the students created drawings and sketches depicting the UFO and the beings they claimed to have seen. These illustrations often showed similar features, reinforcing the consistency of their accounts.

While the witnesses were consistent in their testimonies, sceptics have offered alternative explanations, suggesting that the event could have been a mass hysteria or a misinterpretation of a natural phenomenon. The Ariel School UFO incident remains a significant case in Ufology, often cited as one of the most compelling mass sightings involving children.

It continues to be discussed in documentaries, books, and ufology conferences, contributing to the ongoing debate about the validity of UFO encounters. The Ariel School incident stands out not only for the sheer number of witnesses but also for the detailed and consistent nature of the accounts provided by the young students, making it a unique and thought-provoking case in the study of unidentified flying objects.

O'Hare International Airport UFO sighting, Chicago, Illinois

The 2006 O'Hare International Airport UFO sighting on November 7, 2006, remains one of the intriguing and well-documented incidents in the realm of unidentified flying objects (UFOs). This event took place at O'Hare International Airport in Chicago, Illinois, and involved multiple witnesses, including United Airlines employees and pilots.

Eyewitnesses reported seeing a saucer-shaped craft that was unlit and hovering over one of the airport terminals. The sighting created a stir among those present, as the mysterious object seemed to defy conventional explanations. The craft reportedly remained stationary for a significant period, raising concerns among onlookers about its nature and potential impact on airport operations.

What added credibility to this incident was the fact that it was observed by multiple airline personnel, including pilots and ground staff? These witnesses were trained observers familiar with aircraft and airport operations, lending an air of legitimacy to their accounts. The UFO was described as having a saucer-like shape, which is a common characteristic associated with UFO sightings.

One notable aspect of the O'Hare UFO sighting is that the craft appeared to leave the area in a manner inconsistent with known aviation capabilities. Witnesses reported that the UFO executed a rapid vertical ascent, defying the laws of physics as understood for conventional aircraft. This departure further stoked speculation and interest in the incident.

Following the event, the Federal Aviation Administration (FAA) initially downplayed the incident, stating that there was no evidence of the UFO on radar and that the sighting could be attributed to a weather phenomenon known as a "hole-punch cloud." However, this explanation was met with scepticism, as witnesses insisted that what they saw was a physical craft rather than a natural atmospheric occurrence.

The O'Hare UFO sighting sparked debates and discussions within the UFO community, as well as among the general public. It also led to renewed interest in the government's handling of such sightings and the need for greater transparency in reporting and investigating UFO incidents.

In the years that followed, the O'Hare International Airport UFO sighting continued to be a focal point for UFO researchers and enthusiasts, contributing to ongoing conversations about the existence of extra-terrestrial life and the potential for unidentified aerial phenomena to visit Earth. While sceptics may offer alternative explanations, the 2006 O'Hare UFO incident remains an intriguing chapter in the annals of UFO history.

The USS Nimitz UFO Incident, San Diego, California

The USS Nimitz UFO incident, which occurred on November 14, 2004, off the coast of San Diego, California, is one of the most notable and well-documented encounters involving military personnel and unidentified flying objects (UFOs). The incident involved several pilots from the VFA-41 squadron who were flying Super Hornets from the USS Nimitz, a Nimitz-class aircraft carrier.

The events unfolded when the USS Princeton, a Ticonderoga-class guided-missile cruiser equipped with the advanced Aegis radar system, detected multiple unidentified aerial objects on its radar. The USS Princeton crew members observed these objects exhibiting highly unusual flight characteristics and manoeuvres. The crew reported their findings to the command, and subsequently, the VFA-41 squadron was directed to intercept one of these unidentified flying objects.

The pilots reported a visual encounter with an object that displayed extraordinary capabilities, such as rapid acceleration and sudden changes in direction. They also managed to record an infrared video of the encounter. The infrared footage captured by the Navy personnel became a crucial piece of evidence in the investigation of the incident.

The U.S. Navy officially acknowledged the authenticity of the video and confirmed that it was recorded by Navy personnel during the USS Nimitz encounter. Despite this acknowledgment, the Navy stated that they had not yet identified the nature of the observed phenomena. The term used by the military to describe such occurrences is "unexplained aerial phenomena" (UAP), a phrase introduced to replace the more widely known term "UFO."

The incident gained widespread attention when details were later revealed to the public. It sparked renewed interest in the study of unidentified aerial phenomena and led to discussions about the need for more transparency regarding such encounters. The USS Nimitz UFO incident became a focal point in the broader conversation about unidentified aerial phenomena, drawing attention from both the public and researchers interested in understanding the potential implications of encounters with advanced and unexplained aerial objects.

In subsequent years, the U.S. government has taken steps to declassify and release additional information related to various UFO encounters, signalling a shift towards greater openness on the subject. The USS Nimitz incident remains a prominent case in the ongoing exploration of unidentified aerial phenomena, contributing to the ongoing efforts to better understand these mysterious encounters.

Roswell, New Mexico

No discussion on UFO hotspots would be complete without a nod to Roswell, New Mexico. In 1947, this unassuming town catapulted into the spotlight when reports of a crashed "flying disc" surfaced. The Roswell Incident has since become a cornerstone of UFO lore, spawning numerous conspiracy theories and fueling the fascination surrounding extraterrestrial life.

The mention of UFO hotspots invariably leads to Roswell, New Mexico, a town forever etched in the annals of UFO lore. The year 1947 marked a turning point when the tranquillity of this otherwise unassuming town was disrupted by reports of a crashed "flying disc" near Roswell. The incident, now famously known as the Roswell Incident, thrust Roswell into the spotlight and became a pivotal moment in the history of UFO sightings.

The initial reports of a crashed flying disc were first made public by the Roswell Army Air Field (RAAF), generating widespread speculation and intrigue. The military's initial press release confirmed the discovery of a "flying disc," but shortly afterward, an abrupt reversal occurred, with officials stating that it was, in fact, a weather balloon that had crashed. This abrupt change in the official narrative increased suspicions and ignited a wave of conspiracy theories that persist to this day.

The Roswell Incident has become a cornerstone of UFO mythology, with various accounts and interpretations contributing to its mystique. Numerous witnesses, including military personnel and civilians, claimed to have seen debris scattered across the crash site, describing unusual materials that seemed otherworldly. Some even reported the recovery of small, humanoid bodies near the wreckage, adding an extra layer of intrigue to the unfolding mystery.

In the years that followed, the Roswell Incident garnered attention from UFO researchers, enthusiasts, and sceptics alike. The incident fuelled the growth of the UFO phenomenon in popular culture, inspiring countless books, documentaries, and films that explore the possibility of extra-terrestrial contact. Roswell has become synonymous with government secrecy, cover-ups, and the ongoing search for the truth about unidentified flying objects.

Several official investigations into the Roswell Incident have been conducted over the years, each with varying conclusions. The United States Air Force released two reports in the 1990s, with the first suggesting that the wreckage was from a top-secret project known as Project Mogul, which used high-altitude balloons to detect Soviet nuclear tests. The second report, issued in 1997, concluded that the bodies reported by some witnesses were likely crash test dummies used in military experiments.

Despite these explanations, the Roswell Incident continues to captivate the public imagination, and many remain sceptical of the official accounts. The town of Roswell has embraced its role in UFO history, becoming a focal point for tourists and UFO enthusiasts who visit the International UFO Museum and Research Centre to explore exhibits and learn more about the mysterious events that unfolded in 1947.

The legacy of Roswell endures as an enduring symbol of the enduring fascination with the possibility of extra-terrestrial life and the ongoing quest for answers in the realm of UFO sightings and encounters.

Rendlesham Forest, Suffolk, England

Venturing across the Atlantic, Rendlesham Forest in Suffolk, England, has secured its own unique place in the annals of UFO history. In December 1980, this serene woodland setting became the stage for an enigmatic series of events that would later be known as the Rendlesham Forest incident. The incident unfolded near the RAF Bentwaters base, where military personnel reported encountering strange lights and phenomena, earning Rendlesham Forest the moniker of "Britain's Roswell."

The events transpired over several nights, starting on December 26, 1980, when personnel from the United States Air Force stationed at the dual-use RAF Bentwaters and RAF Woodbridge reported sightings of unusual lights in the forest adjacent to the bases. According to witnesses, the lights were described as bright, colored orbs that exhibited seemingly intelligent and controlled movements.

One of the most compelling aspects of the Rendlesham Forest incident is that military personnel, including deputy base commander Lieutenant Colonel Charles Halt, ventured into the forest to investigate the strange occurrences. During their investigation on the night of December 27, Halt and his team reported witnessing unusual phenomena, including the appearance of unidentified objects, damage to trees, and inexplicable markings on the ground. Halt later documented his experiences in an official memorandum, lending a degree of credibility to the accounts.

The Rendlesham Forest incident quickly garnered attention and has since become one of the most studied and debated UFO cases in the United Kingdom. Numerous theories have been put forth to explain the events, ranging from mundane explanations such as misidentified aircraft or military exercises to more exotic hypotheses involving extraterrestrial visitation.

Researchers and investigators continue to grapple with the perplexing nature of the Rendlesham Forest incident, with differing perspectives on the credibility of eyewitness accounts and the possible explanations for the observed phenomena. The incident remains a focal point for UFO enthusiasts, skeptics, and researchers alike, contributing to the ongoing discourse surrounding unidentified aerial phenomena and extraterrestrial encounters.

In recognition of its significance, Rendlesham Forest has become a destination for those intrigued by UFO history, with guided tours and events organized to explore the locations where the mysterious events unfolded. The enduring mystery of Rendlesham Forest serves as a testament to the enduring fascination with unexplained aerial phenomena and the quest for answers in the realm of UFO encounters on both sides of the Atlantic.

The Frederick Valentich UFO Incident, Bass Strait, Australia

The disappearance of Frederick Valentich is a mysterious incident that occurred on October 21, 1978, over the Bass Strait in Australia. Frederick Valentich, a 20-year-old pilot, was flying a Cessna 182 Skylane from Moorabbin Airport in Melbourne to King Island.

At around 7:06 pm, Valentich contacted Melbourne air traffic control to report an unidentified flying object (UFO) or strange craft that he claimed was following him. He described the craft as having bright lights and said that it was orbiting above him. Valentich reported that the object was moving at high speed and that he was experiencing engine problems.

Valentich's last transmission to air traffic control was chilling. He said, "That strange aircraft is hovering on top of me again ... it is hovering and it's not an aircraft." Following this transmission, communication with Valentich was lost, and neither he nor his aircraft were ever found.

The disappearance sparked widespread speculation and theories, including suggestions of UFO abduction. However, the official investigation by the Australian Department of Transport concluded that the reason for Valentich's disappearance could not be determined. The final report mentioned that the possibility of a hoax or a psychological issue on the part of Valentich could not be ruled out.

The Valentich disappearance has become a notable case in the realm of UFO-related incidents and aviation mysteries. Here are some additional points and aspects of the case:

Official Investigation: The official investigation into Valentich's disappearance was led by the Australian Department of Transport. The final report, released in 1982, did not definitively determine the cause of the incident. The report acknowledged the lack of physical evidence and the mysterious circumstances surrounding the disappearance.

UFO Theories: Given Valentich's descriptions of a strange aircraft and the lack of a conventional explanation, many UFO enthusiasts and conspiracy theorists have speculated that he encountered an unidentified flying object. Some believe that he may have been abducted by extraterrestrial beings.

Skeptical Explanations: Skeptics have proposed alternative explanations for the incident. Some suggest that Valentich may have become disoriented or experienced spatial illusions, leading to his misinterpretation of the events. Others argue that it could have been a deliberate hoax or a staged disappearance.

Other Witness Reports: On the same evening as Valentich's disappearance, there were reports from individuals on the ground who claimed to have seen unusual lights in the sky. However, these reports are subjective and vary in detail.

Psychological Factors: The official investigation raised the possibility of psychological factors contributing to the incident. Valentich was known to be interested in UFOs and had previously made UFO reports. Some have speculated that his beliefs and interests might have influenced his perception of the events.

Legacy: The Valentich case continues to be discussed in books, documentaries, and online forums dedicated to UFO phenomena and unsolved mysteries. It remains a topic of interest for those intrigued by the unknown and unexplained.

Despite the passage of time, the disappearance of Frederick Valentich remains an enduring mystery, and it has contributed to the lore surrounding UFO encounters and unexplained disappearances in aviation history. The lack of concrete evidence and the enigmatic nature of Valentich's last transmissions have kept the case open to various interpretations and speculations.

Hessdalen, Norway

The mysterious phenomenon known as the Hessdalen lights has captivated scientists, researchers, and UFO enthusiasts alike since it was first documented in the early 1980s. The remote valley of Hessdalen, located in central Norway, became the stage for an inexplicable light show featuring bright, floating orbs of light that appeared in various colors and sizes.

These lights, often referred to as unidentified flying objects (UFOs), have sparked numerous scientific investigations in an attempt to unravel the mystery behind their origin.

The lights in Hessdalen are known for their unique characteristics. They manifest as luminous, spherical shapes that hover, move in unpredictable patterns, and sometimes emit peculiar sounds.

Witnesses have reported seeing lights of various colors, including white, yellow, red, and blue. The duration of these sightings can vary, ranging from brief flashes to prolonged displays that last for several hours.

Scientists and researchers have employed a variety of methods to study the Hessdalen lights, including setting up monitoring stations, installing cameras, and conducting regular field observations. One notable effort was the establishment of the Hessdalen Automatic Measurement Station (Hessdalen AMS) in 1998, which aimed to systematically record and analyse data related to the lights. The station recorded valuable information such as the lights' frequency, intensity, and trajectory, but despite these efforts, the source of the phenomenon remains elusive.

Several hypotheses have been proposed to explain the Hessdalen lights, although none have been conclusively proven. Some theories suggest that the lights could be related to ionized gases in the atmosphere, while others speculate about the possibility of extra-terrestrial origins. The rugged terrain and isolated location of Hessdalen make it challenging to conduct comprehensive studies, adding to the mystique surrounding the phenomenon.

One interesting aspect of the research is the collaboration between scientists, local residents, and enthusiasts. The Hessdalen Phenomena Project, initiated in the early 2000s, brought together experts from various disciplines, including physicists, geologists, and astronomers, to investigate the lights collaboratively. This interdisciplinary approach aimed to combine expertise and resources in the pursuit of a clearer understanding of the phenomenon.

Despite decades of investigation, the Hessdalen lights continue to defy explanation, maintaining the valley's status as a global hotspot for UFO sightings. The enigma surrounding these lights not only contributes to ongoing scientific curiosity but also attracts visitors and researchers from around the world who seek to witness the unexplained phenomenon for themselves. As technology advances and research techniques improve, the hope is that one day the secrets of the Hessdalen lights will be unveiled, shedding light on one of the most intriguing mysteries in the field of unexplained aerial phenomena.

The USS Theodore Roosevelt UFO Incident

The USS Theodore Roosevelt UFO incidents, occurring from June 2, 2014, to March 10, 2015, marked a significant period of heightened attention to unexplained aerial phenomena (UAP) within the United States Navy. The events unfolded along the East Coast of the United States, involving Navy pilots stationed on the USS Theodore Roosevelt aircraft carrier.

The genesis of these incidents coincided with an equipment upgrade on the Theodore Roosevelt. Following the upgrade, Navy pilots began to detect unexplained objects on their radar systems. Notably, some pilots reported an inability to visually confirm the presence of these mysterious objects, while others managed to capture video footage of the encounters. This video footage, eventually released to the public, depicted unidentified aerial phenomena exhibiting unusual and highly agile flight characteristics.

Concerned about the nature of these encounters, the Navy pilots reported the incidents to the Advanced Aerospace Threat Identification Program (AATIP). At the time, AATIP was a relatively obscure initiative tasked with investigating and analysing reports of unidentified aerial phenomena. The information provided by the Theodore Roosevelt pilots played a crucial role in bringing attention to the potential security implications of unexplained aerial encounters.

The publicity surrounding the USS Theodore Roosevelt UFO incidents, combined with other similar reports, prompted a reassessment of the military's approach to such phenomena. Subsequently, the Department of Defence (DoD) and the Navy took steps to establish new guidelines and protocols for reporting and investigating unexplained aerial phenomena sightings. This marked a shift toward a more systematic and transparent approach to addressing encounters with unidentified objects in the sky.

The incidents on the USS Theodore Roosevelt brought the topic of UAP into the public spotlight, sparking discussions about the need for increased research, cooperation between government agencies, and a more open discourse on the subject. The developments during this period laid the groundwork for subsequent revelations and ongoing efforts to better understand the nature of unidentified aerial phenomena and their potential implications for national security.

Hoia Baciu Forest, Romania

Stepping into the realms of Eastern Europe, the Hoia Baciu Forest in Romania emerges as a captivating enigma, earning itself the ominous title of the "Bermuda Triangle of Transylvania." This haunting woodland, located near the city of Cluj-Napoca, has gained notoriety for its plethora of unsettling tales involving mysterious disappearances, unexplained electronic malfunctions, and purported encounters with unidentified beings. The forest's eerie reputation has lured inquisitive researchers and thrill-seekers alike, each hoping to unravel the mysteries concealed within its shadowy depths.

The Hoia Baciu Forest's reputation for the paranormal can be traced back decades, with stories of strange occurrences capturing the imagination of locals and visitors alike. One of the most notable legends revolves around a shepherd who, along with his flock, vanished without a trace in the forest. This tale, along with other accounts of inexplicable phenomena, has contributed to the forest's mystique and earned it comparisons to the infamous Bermuda Triangle.

Numerous witnesses have reported encountering bizarre phenomena within the forest's boundaries. Visitors claim to have experienced electronic devices malfunctioning unexpectedly, including cameras and compasses behaving erratically. Additionally, there are reports of individuals feeling an overwhelming sense of anxiety or nausea, further fueling the forest's reputation as a place imbued with peculiar energies.

Perhaps the most chilling aspect of the Hoia Baciu Forest is the reported sightings of strange apparitions and unidentified beings. Witnesses describe encounters with ghostly figures, mysterious orbs of light, and even humanoid entities. These accounts have led some to speculate that the forest may serve as a portal to other dimensions or a focal point for paranormal activity.

In response to the intriguing tales surrounding Hoia Baciu, researchers and paranormal investigators have delved into the mysteries concealed within the forest. Expeditions and studies have been conducted to capture evidence of the reported phenomena, ranging from electromagnetic anomalies to unusual patterns in plant growth. Despite these efforts, the forest continues to guard its secrets, leaving researchers with more questions than answers.

Hoia Baciu Forest's allure persists as a destination for those drawn to the unexplained, with guided tours offered to those eager to explore its haunted trails. The forest stands as a testament to the enduring fascination with the supernatural and the unknown, as well as the human desire to uncover the mysteries that shroud certain places in an air of enigmatic uncertainty. The "Bermuda Triangle of Transylvania" remains a captivating enigma, beckoning the curious to venture into its depths in search of answers.

The Ilkley Moor UFO Incident, UK

The Ilkley Moor UFO incident, which occurred on December 1, 1987, is an intriguing event that took place on Ilkley Moor in the United Kingdom. The incident involved a retired police officer named Philip Spencer, who claimed to have captured a photograph of a mysterious being on the moor.

On that fateful day, Spencer was exploring the area when he encountered an unusual sight. He quickly took out his camera and managed to photograph what he described as a strange being. According to Spencer's account, the being seemed to be aware of being photographed and promptly fled the scene. The mysterious entity was said to have departed in a domed craft, leaving behind a trail of curiosity and speculation.

The photograph taken by Spencer added a visual element to the account, further fueling discussions and debates surrounding the Ilkley Moor incident. The incident became a point of interest for both UFO enthusiasts and skeptics alike, as it joined the ranks of numerous other reported sightings and encounters around the world.

As with many UFO incidents, the Ilkley Moor case sparked various theories and interpretations. Some believed that the being captured in the photograph was an extraterrestrial entity, while others suggested more conventional explanations, such as a misidentification of a natural or man-made object. Skeptics questioned the authenticity of the photograph and raised doubts about the credibility of the witness.

In the aftermath of the Ilkley Moor UFO incident, investigations and discussions persisted within both UFO research circles and the general public. One aspect that intrigued many was the character of Philip Spencer, the retired police officer who claimed to have witnessed and photographed the strange being on the moor.

Spencer's credibility came under scrutiny, as is customary in UFO and paranormal cases. Skeptics questioned the authenticity of the photograph, highlighting potential alternative explanations such as photographic anomalies, hoaxes, or misinterpretations of mundane objects. Additionally, the fact that Spencer was a retired police officer added an interesting layer to the narrative, with some arguing that his background in law enforcement could either bolster or undermine the credibility of his account, depending on one's perspective.

The Ilkley Moor incident also prompted broader discussions about the nature of UFO sightings and encounters. Some researchers and enthusiasts saw it as another piece of evidence supporting the existence of extraterrestrial life and their occasional visits to Earth. Others were more cautious, emphasizing the need for rigorous scientific investigation and critical analysis to separate genuine unexplained phenomena from misidentifications or hoaxes.

In the years following the incident, the photograph taken by Spencer underwent various analyses, ranging from amateur examinations to more formal investigations by UFO research organizations. However, definitive conclusions about the nature of the being in the photograph remained elusive. The lack of concrete evidence left the Ilkley Moor incident in a realm of uncertainty, where belief systems, personal biases, and the ongoing mystery of UFO phenomena played a significant role in shaping individual interpretations.

The Ilkley Moor UFO incident serves as a reminder of the enduring fascination and mystery surrounding unidentified flying objects. Whether seen as evidence of extraterrestrial visitation or a case yet to be explained by more conventional means, the incident remains an intriguing chapter in the complex tapestry of UFO lore, inviting ongoing scrutiny and speculation from both believers and skeptics alike.

The Arequipa UFO Incident, Peru

The Arequipa UFO incident of April 11, 1980, gained notoriety due to its military involvement and the detailed account provided by fighter pilot Oscar Santa María Huertas. Here's an expanded overview of the incident:

Background: In the early morning hours of April 11, 1980, La Joya Air Force Base in Peru received reports of an unidentified flying object (UFO) in restricted airspace. In response to this, fighter pilot Oscar Santa María Huertas was scrambled to intercept and investigate the mysterious aerial phenomenon.

The Encounter: Upon reaching the location, Huertas engaged the UFO in his Sukhoi Su-22 fighter jet. In an attempt to identify or neutralize the object, he reportedly fired a barrage of 30mm shells at it. Despite the attack, Huertas claimed that the UFO showed no signs of damage and instead ascended rapidly to an altitude of 19,200 meters.

Description of the UFO: Huertas provided a detailed description of the UFO, likening its shape to that of an incandescent lightbulb. Notably, he emphasized a wider circular silver base. What intrigued investigators and UFO enthusiasts was Huertas' assertion that the object lacked conventional aircraft components. According to his account, the UFO had no wings, propulsion jets, exhaust systems, windows, antennae, or any other discernible features typically associated with man-made aircraft.

Speculations and Investigations: The incident sparked various speculations about the nature of the UFO. Some proponents of extraterrestrial theories pointed to the unconventional characteristics described by Huertas, suggesting that it might be evidence of advanced alien technology. Skeptics, on the other hand, proposed alternative explanations such as misidentifications of natural phenomena, experimental military aircraft, or technical malfunctions.

Legacy and Ongoing Debates: The Arequipa UFO incident remains a notable event in the realm of unidentified aerial phenomena (UAP). Despite investigations and discussions, no conclusive explanation has been provided for the object encountered by Huertas. The incident contributes to the broader debate on the existence and origins of UFOs, with believers arguing for the possibility of extraterrestrial visitations, and skeptics urging a more cautious and grounded approach to interpreting such sightings.

In the decades since the event, the Arequipa UFO incident has become a case frequently cited in UFO literature and discussions surrounding the unexplained aerial phenomena, adding to the intrigue and mystery that often surrounds such encounters.

The Socorro UFO Incident, New Mexico

In the annals of UFO encounters, the Socorro UFO incident of April 1964 stands out as a compelling and perplexing case. This incident unfolded in the small town of Socorro, New Mexico, when police officer Lonnie Zamora had an otherworldly experience that would become one of the most investigated and discussed UFO sightings in history.

On the evening of April 24, 1964, Officer Zamora was on duty, patrolling the outskirts of Socorro. As he followed a speeding car, he heard a loud roar and saw a flame in the sky. Assuming it was an explosion or a car crash, Zamora abandoned the pursuit and headed towards the source of the disturbance.

To his astonishment, Zamora came across a metallic, egg-shaped craft on the ground, surrounded by a bluish flame. The object was unlike any aircraft he had ever seen, and it displayed no visible means of propulsion or wings. As Zamora approached, he observed two humanoid figures near the craft.

The beings were described as small, with white coveralls and helmets, and they appeared not to notice Zamora initially. Startled by his presence, one of the beings turned and looked at him before both quickly entered the craft. The object then emitted a loud, roaring sound and ascended vertically before disappearing from sight.

What sets the Socorro UFO incident apart is the credibility of the witness, Lonnie Zamora. As a police officer with a reputation for integrity, Zamora was considered a reliable and trustworthy observer. Additionally, the case was extensively investigated by authorities, including the U.S. Air Force and Project Blue Book, the official government study of UFOs at the time.

Physical evidence, such as ground imprints and burned vegetation at the landing site, added a layer of complexity to the Socorro incident. The investigation confirmed that the soil exhibited unusual characteristics, and the burn marks on the plants were consistent with Zamora's account.

Despite the thorough investigation, no conclusive explanation was reached. The U.S. Air Force classified the case as an "unknown" in their final Project Blue Book report, leaving the incident officially unexplained.

The Socorro UFO incident has since become a focal point for UFO researchers and enthusiasts, sparking debates and discussions about the nature of the encounter and its potential implications. Lonnie Zamora's detailed and consistent account, coupled with the physical evidence, continues to contribute to the broader tapestry of UFO encounters and remains a topic of interest for those intrigued by the unexplained.

The Cerrik UFO Incident, Elbasan, Albania

The Cerrik UFO incident that occurred on July 12, 1993, in Cërrik, Elbasan, Albania, is a fascinating event that captured the attention of the local population and law enforcement. Around 8:00 pm, residents were startled as a glowing flying object appeared in the evening sky. Eyewitnesses described the illuminated object as making sudden and quick movements, defying the typical patterns of conventional aircraft.

As word quickly spread throughout the town about the unidentified flying object, it prompted concern and curiosity among the residents. Law enforcement was notified, and they took measures to limit the spread of panic among the population. Dealing with situations involving potential unknown aerial phenomena is often challenging, as authorities must balance public safety with the need for accurate information.

Throughout the incident, eyewitness accounts provided a variety of descriptions, further adding to the mystery surrounding the event. The glowing object reportedly exhibited behaviors that were inconsistent with known aircraft or celestial bodies. The sudden appearance and disappearance of the UFO within a span of two hours added an air of intrigue and uncertainty.

Investigations into such incidents are often complex, as identifying the nature of the flying object can be challenging. In many cases, sightings of unidentified flying objects lead to speculation and discussions about extraterrestrial phenomena, adding an element of wonder and speculation to the local community and beyond.

Ultimately, the Cerrik UFO incident remains an unsolved mystery, and it serves as a reminder of the ongoing fascination and intrigue surrounding unidentified flying objects and their potential implications. The event likely sparked continued interest and discussions within the community and possibly contributed to broader conversations about the existence of extraterrestrial life and the mysteries of the cosmos.

The Belgian UFO Wave

The Belgian UFO wave of the late 1980s is one of the most intriguing and well-documented series of UFO sightings in modern history. From 1989 to 1990, Belgium became the epicenter of an unprecedented wave of unidentified flying object sightings that captured the attention of the public, the media, and even military authorities. The events unfolded over several months, involving multiple witnesses, radar tracking, and official investigations. This phenomenon remains a subject of debate, speculation, and fascination within the realm of ufology.

Belgium, a small European country nestled between France, Germany, and the Netherlands, is not typically associated with UFO sightings. However, in the late 1980s, the country found itself thrust into the international spotlight due to a series of extraordinary events involving mysterious lights in the sky.

The first notable incident occurred on the night of November 29, 1989, when numerous witnesses reported seeing a large, triangular-shaped object with three bright lights hovering silently in the sky. The object was described as massive, estimated to be about the size of a football field. Witnesses, including police officers, reported that the lights emitted a soft, white glow and were unlike anything they had seen before.

As reports of the sightings flooded in, the Belgian military became increasingly concerned about the nature of these mysterious objects. On the night of March 30, 1990, two Belgian Air Force F-16 fighter jets were scrambled to investigate a radar-confirmed sighting of an unidentified object. The pilots reported seeing a large, dark triangular object with bright lights at each corner. Despite their attempts to intercept the object, it displayed incredible maneuverability, easily outmaneuvering the fighter jets.

One of the most compelling aspects of the Belgian UFO wave was the radar confirmation of the unidentified objects. The Belgian Air Force's radar systems picked up the presence of unknown craft during several of the sightings. The radar data indicated that these objects were capable of rapid acceleration, sudden stops, and maneuvers that defied the laws of conventional aviation.

While sightings of UFOs often lack concrete evidence, the Belgian UFO wave stands out due to the availability of photographic documentation. Multiple witnesses managed to capture images of the triangular objects using cameras and camcorders. These images, while often blurry and inconclusive, contribute to the overall body of evidence supporting the reality of the sightings.

In response to the growing public interest and concern, the Belgian government took the unusual step of officially investigating the UFO wave. The task force, known as the "UFO Cell," was established to collect and analyze data related to the sightings. The cell included military personnel, police officers, and scientists, all working together to unravel the mystery.

The UFO Cell's investigation produced a detailed report commonly referred to as the "Condon Report," named after Colonel Wilfried De Brouwer, who led the inquiry. The report concluded that the sightings were genuine and not easily explainable by conventional means. It acknowledged the existence of unidentified flying objects but stopped short of attributing them to extraterrestrial origin.

While the Condon Report validated the reality of the sightings, it did not definitively explain the origin of the mysterious objects. Various hypotheses were proposed, including experimental military aircraft, atmospheric phenomena, and even psychological factors. Skeptics argued that the sightings could be attributed to misinterpretations, hoaxes, or natural phenomena.

One intriguing aspect of the Belgian UFO wave is the consideration of the psychosocial hypothesis. Some researchers proposed that the sightings were not solely the result of external phenomena but were influenced by a combination of psychological, social, and cultural factors. This theory suggests that a collective mindset, fueled by media coverage and cultural influences, may have contributed to the perception of UFOs.

The Belgian UFO wave garnered international attention, with media outlets around the world covering the mysterious sightings. The events sparked renewed interest in UFO phenomena globally and prompted discussions about the need for increased transparency and cooperation among nations in investigating such incidents.

Decades after the Belgian UFO wave, the events of 1989-1990 continue to capture the imagination of UFO enthusiasts, researchers, and the curious public. The sightings remain one of the well-documented and perplexing episodes in the history of ufology, prompting ongoing debates about the nature of the unidentified objects and the possible implications for our understanding of extraterrestrial life.

The Belgian UFO wave of the late 1980s remains a fascinating chapter in the annals of UFO research. The convergence of eyewitness accounts, radar data, military involvement, and photographic evidence creates a compelling narrative that defies easy explanation. Whether viewed as a collective delusion, a series of misidentifications, or genuine encounters with unknown phenomena, the events in Belgium during that period have left an indelible mark on the field of ufology. As we continue to explore the mysteries of the cosmos, the Belgian UFO wave serves as a reminder that there is much about our universe that remains unknown and that the quest for understanding extends beyond the bounds of our terrestrial home.

Skinwalker Ranch, Utah, USA

Skinwalker Ranch, located in the Uintah Basin of northeastern Utah, has gained notoriety as one of the most mysterious and reportedly active UFO hot spots in the world. The ranch has a rich history of paranormal phenomena, including UFO sightings, strange creatures, crop circles, and unexplained scientific anomalies. The name "Skinwalker" itself is derived from Navajo folklore, referring to shape-shifting witches or beings with the ability to transform into animals.

The ranch was initially known as the Sherman Ranch, named after its owners, the Sherman family, who first reported unusual and perplexing occurrences on the property in the 1990s. The Shermans claimed to have witnessed everything from unidentified flying objects and strange lights in the sky to encounters with bizarre creatures, including large wolves and other anomalous entities.

One of the most intriguing aspects of Skinwalker Ranch is its association with the Defense Intelligence Agency (DIA) and the

Advanced Aerospace Threat Identification Program (AATIP). The AATIP, a secret government initiative, was established to investigate unidentified aerial phenomena (UAP), commonly known as UFOs. Reports suggest that the AATIP had an interest in the ranch due to the high number of reported UFO sightings and other unexplained phenomena.

In addition to UFO sightings, witnesses have reported strange occurrences such as mutilated cattle, unusual electromagnetic fields, and portals or doorways to other dimensions. The scientific community remains skeptical, and the lack of concrete evidence has led some to dismiss the claims as mere hoaxes or exaggerations. However, the reputation of Skinwalker Ranch continues to attract researchers, paranormal enthusiasts, and even documentary filmmakers eager to explore the mysteries surrounding the area.

Notably, Skinwalker Ranch gained widespread attention through books, documentaries, and media coverage. The most prominent work is the book "Hunt for the Skinwalker" by investigative journalist George Knapp and biochemist Colm Kelleher, who conducted scientific investigations on the ranch. The book details their experiences and the strange phenomena witnessed during their time on the property.

The ranch has changed ownership multiple times, with the most recent owner being Brandon Fugal, a Utah-based businessman. Fugal has continued to explore the mysteries of the ranch and has allowed some level of scientific investigation, albeit with limited public access.

While the legends and stories surrounding Skinwalker Ranch remain controversial, the location continues to be a focal point for those intrigued by the unexplained and the possibility of encountering extraterrestrial or paranormal phenomena. The mystique of Skinwalker Ranch persists, making it a subject of ongoing fascination and speculation within both the UFO community and popular culture.

The Phoenix Lights Incident, Arizona, USA

The Phoenix Lights incident, which occurred on March 13, 1997, remains one of the most famous and widely debated UFO sightings in modern history. The event involved a series of unexplained lights that were observed in the night sky over Phoenix, Arizona, and various other parts of the state. Witnesses reported seeing a formation of lights in a V-shape or triangular pattern, silently gliding across the sky.

The event unfolded in two distinct phases. The first phase involved a series of lights that appeared over the city of Phoenix, moving in a slow and deliberate manner. The lights were described by witnesses as large, bright, and stationary, forming a distinct pattern in the night sky. The second phase occurred later in the evening and involved a massive triangular formation of lights that moved across the state of Arizona, covering a vast distance.

Thousands of people reported seeing the lights, including residents, pilots, and law enforcement officials. The sightings prompted a significant response from the public, the media, and government authorities. In the aftermath of the incident, the U.S. Air Force initially suggested that the lights were flares dropped by A-10 Warthog aircraft during a training exercise at the Barry M. Goldwater Range. However, many witnesses contested this explanation, arguing that the lights they observed were too large, too bright, and moved in a manner inconsistent with flares.

The Phoenix Lights incident gained widespread attention and sparked a renewed interest in UFO phenomena. The government's official explanation did not satisfy many skeptics, and the incident continues to be a subject of speculation, debate, and investigation within the UFO research community. Some researchers and witnesses believe that the lights were of extraterrestrial origin, while others propose alternative explanations, such as advanced military aircraft or experimental technology.

In subsequent years, the Phoenix Lights incident has become a focal point for UFO enthusiasts and researchers, with annual commemorations taking place in Phoenix to mark the anniversary of the event. The incident has also been the subject of documentaries, books, and television programs, contributing to its enduring legacy in the realm of UFO folklore and conspiracy theories. Despite ongoing interest, a conclusive explanation for the Phoenix Lights remains elusive, adding to the mystery and intrigue surrounding this notable UFO sighting.

Stadio Artemi Franchi UFO Incident, Tuscany, Italy

Seventy years ago a football match ground to a halt when unidentified flying objects were spotted above a stadium in Florence. Did aliens come to earth? If not, what were they?

It was 27 October 1954, a typically crisp autumn day in Tuscany. The mighty Fiorentina club was playing against its local rival Pistoiese.

Ten-thousand fans were watching in the concrete bowl of the Stadio Artemi Franchi. But just after half-time the stadium fell eerily silent - then a roar went up from the crowd. The spectators were no longer watching the match, but were looking up at the sky, fingers pointing. The players stopped playing, the ball rolled to a stand-still.

One of the footballers on the pitch was Ardico Magnini - he was something of a legend at the club and had played for Italy at the 1954 World Cup.

"I remember everything from A to Z," he says. "It was something that looked like an egg that was moving slowly, slowly, slowly. Everyone was looking up and also there was some glitter coming down from the sky, silver glitter.

"We were astonished we had never seen anything like it before. We were absolutely shocked."

Among the crowd was Gigi Boni, a lifelong Fiorentina fan. "I remember clearly seeing this incredible sight," he says. His description of multiple objects differs slightly from Magnini's.

"They were moving very fast and then they just stopped. It all lasted a couple of minutes. I would like to describe them as being like Cuban cigars. They just reminded me of Cuban cigars, in the way they looked."

Boni has spent many years reliving that day in his mind. "I think they were extra-terrestrial. That's what I believe, and there's no other explanation I can give myself."

Another of the players, Romolo Tuci, still sprightly in his 80s, agrees. "In those years everybody was talking about aliens, everybody was talking UFOs and we had the experience, we saw them, we saw them directly, for real."

The incident at the stadium cannot simply be interpreted as mass hysteria - there were numerous UFO sightings in many towns across Tuscany that day and over the days that followed. According to some eyewitness accounts a ray of white light was seen in the sky coming from Prato, north of Florence.

Another man who relishes the chance to speak about that day is Roberto Pinotti, the president of Italy's National UFO Centre. He has written many books about UFOs and his home in the centre of Florence is stuffed full of alien memorabilia, posters of old Italian B-movies, framed newspaper articles and black-and-white photographs of blurry flying saucers.

"The players and the public were stunned seeing these objects above the stadium," Pinotti says.

"At the time the newspapers spoke of aliens from Mars. Of course now we know that is not so - but we may conclude that it was an intelligent phenomenon, a technological phenomenon and a phenomenon that cannot be linked with anything we know on Earth."

He's also intrigued by the material that fell from the sky - what Magnini describes as silver glitter.

"A wave of flying saucers over Italy," reported the Domenica del Corriere three years later.

"It is a fact that at the same time the UFOs were seen over Florence there was a strange, sticky substance falling from above. In English we call this 'angel hair'," says Pinotti.

"The only problem is after a short period of time it disintegrates." As a 10-year-old-boy he witnessed this phenomenon himself. "I remember, in broad daylight, seeing the roofs of the houses in Florence covered in this white substance for one hour and, like snow, it just evaporated.

"No-one knows what this strange substance has to do with UFOs."

Variously described by witnesses as similar to cotton wool or cobwebs, the substance was hard to collect because it disintegrated on contact - but some people were determined to find out what it was.

One of them was a journalist at the Florentine newspaper La Nazione, the late Giorgio Batini. In 2003 he told an Italian television programme, Voyager, how on that day he received hundreds of phone calls about the sightings. From the offices of La Nazione in the centre of town his own view of the sky was blocked by the Cathedral, so he went up to the top of the newspaper's building to see what everyone was talking about. The 81-year-old recalled seeing "shiny balls" moving fast towards the dome of the Cathedral.

Batini ventured out to investigate. He came across a wood outside the city that was covered in the white fluff. He gathered several samples by rolling them up on a matchstick, and took them to the Institute of Chemical Analysis at the University of Florence. When he got there he found that others had done the same.

The lab, led by respected scientist Prof Giovanni Canneri, subjected the material to spectrographic analysis and concluded that it contained the elements boron, silicon, calcium and magnesium, and that it was not radioactive. Unfortunately this did not provide any conclusive answers - and the material was destroyed in the process.

Could it have come from a UFO? "It's an absolutely silly idea. Science totally rejects this idea," says US Air Force pilot-turned-astronomer James McGaha. From the Grasslands Observatory in South Eastern Arizona he has spent more than 40,000 hours staring at the night sky. Not to mention the additional hours he's spent in the cockpit of US fighter jets.

"You know the whole UFO phenomenon is nothing but myth, magic and superstition, wrapped up in this idea that somehow aliens are coming here either to save us or destroy us," he says.

In McGaha's view, the whole spectacle, "angel hair" and all, was nothing more than migrating spiders.

"When I looked at this case originally I thought perhaps it was a fireball, a very bright meteor breaking up in the atmosphere. They can be cigar-shaped with pieces breaking off. But it became fairly apparent that this was actually caused by young spiders spinning webs, very, very thin webs.

"The spiders use these webs as sails and they link together and you get a big glob of this stuff in the sky and the spiders ride on this to move between locations. They just fly on the wind and these things have been recorded at 14,000 feet above the ground. So, when the sunlight glistens off this, you get all kinds of visual effects.

"As some of this stuff breaks off and falls to the ground, this all seems magical of course," says McGaha. "But I'm fairly confident that's what happened that day."

This theory is backed up by the fact that September and October are the months when spiders in the northern hemisphere migrate - and spectacular spider migrations still make headlines today. But it hasn't convinced everyone.

"Of course I know about the migrating spiders hypothesis - it's pure nonsense. It's an old story and also a stupid story," says Pinotti.

He disputes the spider theory because of the chemical analysis of the "angel hair" samples. Spider silk is a protein - an organic compound containing nitrogen, calcium, hydrogen and oxygen - not the elements reportedly found in the samples Batini and others brought to the university.

Seventy years on, the chances of determining the cause of the incident are slim. "I wouldn't trust any reports of an old and strange event like this unless I'd seen the data," says science writer Philip Ball. He agrees that the elements said to have been observed in the "angel hair" don't seem to tally with the spider theory.

"Magnesium and calcium are fairly common elements in living bodies, boron and silicon much less so - but if these were the main elements that the white fluff contained, it doesn't sound to me as though they'd come from spiders," he says.

So it all remains a mystery. No matter what the scientists say, those who were there are convinced that what they saw was unlike anything on earth.

Romolo Tuci just feels lucky to have been there. His eyes dance excitedly as he remembers that curious day. "I was spell-bound and I was also so, so happy."

As we navigate through these diverse UFO hotspots, patterns begin to emerge, suggesting that the allure of the unknown transcends cultural and geographic boundaries. The Falkirk Triangle stands not alone but as a thread in the intricate fabric of global mysteries, inviting us to continue our quest for understanding in the vast cosmos beyond.

CHAPTER SIX

Government Involvement Worldwide

The Bonnybridge UFO incidents have been a subject of fascination and speculation for years. Multiple UFO sightings in the area prompted responses from local authorities and governmental bodies, as the phenomenon garnered attention not only from the public but also from the media. There is also the added dimension of authenticity when factoring in the 2023 bombshell revelations from US military whistleblowers Grusch, Fravor and Graves.

In scenes that felt reminiscent of a science-fiction movie, the US Congress held a public hearing on claims the government was covering up its knowledge of UFOs.

Unsurprisingly, the hearing generated huge interest in the US and around the world as it heard from three key witnesses, including David Grusch, a whistleblower former intelligence official who in June claimed the US has possession of "intact and partially intact" alien vehicles.

UFOs have become a high-profile news story in recent years. The US military says it is actively trying to investigate the small number of sightings for which there is no obvious explanation.

As the hearing unfolded there were no new revelations about aliens, but there were startling allegations from witnesses, and a general sense that a cover-up exists somewhere in the US government – as well as skepticism that that has anything to do with "little green men".

The US government conducted a "multi-decade" program which collected, and attempted to reverse-engineer, crashed UFOs, David Grusch told the hearing. Grusch, who led analysis of unexplained anomalous phenomena (UAP) within a US Department of Defense agency until 2023, claimed he had been denied access to secret government UFO programs, said he has faced "very brutal" retaliation as a result of his allegations. He claimed he had knowledge of "people who have been harmed or injured" in the course of government efforts to conceal UFO information.

Congressman Tim Burchett asked Grusch if he has any personal knowledge of people who have been harmed or injured in efforts to cover up or conceal extraterrestrial technology.

Grusch replied: "Yes."

Burchett then asked Grusch if he has heard of anyone being murdered. The former intelligence official answered: "I directed people with that knowledge to the appropriate authorities."

But the Pentagon has denied Grusch's claims of a cover-up. In a statement, a defense department spokesperson said investigators had not discovered "any verifiable information to substantiate claims that any programs regarding the possession or reverse-engineering of extraterrestrial materials have existed in the past or exist currently".

Other witnesses at the hearing were David Fravor, a former navy commander who recalled seeing a strange object in the sky while on a training mission in 2004. Ryan Graves, a retired navy pilot who has since founded Americans for Safe Aerospace, a UAP non-profit, claimed that he saw UAP off the Atlantic coast "every day for at least a couple years".

These reports chime with the Bonnybridge incidents. Local authorities, including the police and government officials, took the Bonnybridge UFO reports seriously. The unusual nature and consistency of the sightings compelled them to investigate, addressing the concerns of residents and ensuring public safety. Police officers were often dispatched to investigate reported sightings, aiming to verify the legitimacy of the claims and to maintain order in the community.

Indeed, Councillor Billy Buchanan has taken these sightings seriously since 1992 to the present day. He has written to all the Prime Ministers of the UK, seeking an enquiry. He has met a stone-wall of silence, but for the standard response from government departments.

Recognizing the complexity of the UFO phenomenon, local authorities occasionally collaborated with UFO researchers and investigators. This collaborative approach aimed to bring a scientific perspective to the observations, separating credible reports from potential hoaxes or misidentifications. Such collaborations also helped authorities manage the public's expectations and fostered a sense of transparency in their investigative efforts.

The ongoing reports of UFO sightings had a noticeable impact on the local community. Residents were both intrigued and concerned, leading to heightened emotions and a sense of urgency for authorities to address the situation. Balancing public perception, preventing panic, and providing accurate information became significant challenges for local authorities throughout the course of these incidents.

In response to the growing interest and concerns surrounding the Bonnybridge sightings, the British government took notice. The Ministry of Defence (MoD) acknowledged that they had received reports of UAP in the area but downplayed the significance, attributing most sightings to conventional phenomena such as aircraft, weather balloons, or natural atmospheric occurrences. However, this official stance did little to quell public curiosity and speculation.

The speculative link between government involvement particularly that of the Ministry of Defence (MOD), and UFO sightings in Bonnybridge has fuelled an undercurrent of mystery and intrigue surrounding the Falkirk Triangle. As eyewitness accounts continue to describe unexplained aerial phenomena in the skies above this Scottish town, theories persist about whether official government entities have actively investigated or monitored these occurrences.

Reports from eyewitnesses often mention sightings of not only unconventional lights and shapes but also the presence of military aircraft in the vicinity. This has led to conjecture that the MOD might have knowledge about the nature of these unidentified objects, prompting questions about the government's level of involvement in studying or even concealing information about these phenomena.

The history of government response to UFO sightings in the United Kingdom adds a layer of complexity to the narrative. While the MOD operated a UFO desk until 2009, its publicly released documents often provided prosaic explanations for reported sightings. The closure of the UFO desk was framed as a response to the declining number of reports and the conclusion that UFO sightings did not present a threat to national security.

However, sceptics argue that the closure of the public-facing UFO desk may not necessarily reflect a cessation of government interest or investigation. Instead, it might signal a shift in strategy, with classified efforts continuing behind closed doors.

Conspiracy theories have emerged, suggesting that the MOD possesses information about advanced technology or extra-terrestrial phenomena observed in the Falkirk Triangle. Some speculate that the government intentionally withholds such information from the public due to concerns about potential social or geopolitical repercussions.

To delve deeper into the alleged government involvement in Bonnybridge's UFO phenomena, one would need access to classified documents and information, which are typically not accessible to the public. Researchers and UFO enthusiasts have periodically submitted Freedom of Information Act requests to obtain documents related to UFO sightings, but the extent of information released and any potential redactions remain subjects of contention.

As public interest persists and the allure of the Falkirk Triangle endures, the question of government involvement in Bonnybridge's UFO mysteries remains an enigma. Whether the government possesses knowledge beyond what has been publicly disclosed and the true extent of its interest in the unexplained phenomena above Bonnybridge continue to be subjects of speculation, contributing to the enduring mystique of this Scottish town.

The involvement of government entities, particularly the Ministry of Defence (MOD), in the UFO phenomena around Bonnybridge has been a subject of intrigue and speculation. Reports and claims of mysterious sightings in the skies above the Falkirk Triangle have led to questions about whether the government has taken an active interest in investigating these occurrences. In various instances, eyewitnesses have alleged that military aircraft have been observed in the vicinity of reported UFO sightings, raising suspicions about the government's awareness and potential surveillance of the phenomenon. Some locals have suggested that the Ministry of Defence may possess classified information about these occurrences, and that there could be a deliberate effort to keep such information from the public. Conspiracy theories have circulated, proposing that the MOD has conducted covert investigations into the Bonnybridge UFO phenomena. These theories suggest that government agencies might be in possession of advanced knowledge about the nature of these unidentified aerial phenomena and their potential implications.

Historically, governments worldwide, including the UK, have had policies related to the investigation of UFO sightings. The UK Ministry of Defence maintained a UFO desk until 2009, tasked with collecting and analysing reports of UFO sightings. The released documents from this period, however, often contained mundane explanations for reported phenomena, such as misidentifications of conventional aircraft, weather balloons, or astronomical events. It's crucial to note that official statements from the government often emphasized that the majority of reported sightings had conventional explanations and did not pose a threat to national security. Nonetheless, the persistent rumours and eyewitness accounts in Bonnybridge have ignited ongoing speculation about the extent of government involvement in understanding the mysterious occurrences in the Falkirk Triangle. To gain a comprehensive understanding of any government involvement in Bonnybridge UFO sightings, one would need access to classified documents, which are typically not publicly disclosed.

However, in a bizarre twist and U-turn on Talk TV in 2023, Nick Pope (the MOD's chief public) publically apologised to the people of Bonnybridge, and in particular, Billy Buchanan, stating: In response, Mr Pope categorically denies that he is still working for the government on the UFO issue.

He said: "I think the accusations stem in part from the fact that those of us who have been involved in handling the UFO issue from within the government are automatically going to be the villains in the minds of people who think there's a conspiracy to cover-up the truth about UFOs.

"I understand Billy Buchanan's frustration, because it's true that it was MoD policy for decades to play down the true extent of our interest and involvement in UFOs, and to fob people off with standard responses telling them the subject was of little or no defence significance.

"But this downplaying wasn't to cover up an alien presence, and simply reflected our corporate embarrassment that some UFO sightings suggested the presence of objects in UK airspace capable of speeds, manoeuvres and accelerations that exceeded our own capabilities, yet remained unidentified."

While acknowledging that he can't speak for the MoD, Nick Pope told the programme that as an individual he was happy to apologise.

"Billy Buchanan, the local people in Bonnybridge, perhaps the British people as a whole deserve a corporate apology. I don't buy into every conspiracy theory on UFO's but it was policy for decades to play down all of this."

But Councillor Billy Buchanan dismissed the apology, claiming that Pope is an "agent provocateur", still working for the government.

He said: "After years of working as a debunker for the MOD and giving no credibility to me and my constituents over the years, this individual has now changed his colours by appearing on all programmes and documentaries telling us that aliens are here.

"This incredulous change of course leads me to believe he is an agent provocateur – still working for the government but giving out false information to keep clouding the facts.

"Yes, I am pleased that after years of negativity towards me he has actually apologised to me but more importantly to the people of my area."

National government agencies, particularly the Ministry of Defense (MoD) in the United Kingdom, often became involved in UFO investigations. In the case of Bonnybridge, the MoD acknowledged having examined the reports, sparking interest in the official response to the sightings at a national level. Government agencies played a crucial role in coordinating efforts, collecting data, and attempting to provide explanations for the observed phenomena.

The Freedom of Information Act (FOIA) serves as a vital instrument in promoting government transparency and accountability. This legislation empowers individuals to request access to government records, shedding light on various aspects of governance, including investigations into unexplained phenomena such as UFO sightings.

Over the years, UFO enthusiasts, researchers, and journalists have utilized FOIA requests to access classified government documents related to UFO sightings and investigations. The declassification of such documents has been a transformative force in the study of UFOs, offering the public a glimpse into the official response and decision-making processes of government agencies.

Declassified documents obtained through FOIA requests have played a significant role in shaping public discourse on UFOs. Governments, including the United States, have, at times, declassified certain UFO-related documents, contributing to a more open dialogue about these phenomena. However, the extent of information disclosed varies, and governments often cite national security concerns as a reason for redacting sensitive details.

While FOIA requests have been instrumental in uncovering information, challenges persist. Governments may redact sensitive information, leading to incomplete disclosures. Additionally, the interpretation of released documents may vary, fueling ongoing debates about the true extent of government knowledge regarding UFOs. This has led to calls for greater transparency and the release of more comprehensive information to the public.

The Bonnybridge UFO incidents provide a compelling case study of how local and national authorities respond to unexplained phenomena. Simultaneously, FOIA requests and declassified documents offer a window into the official handling of such cases, contributing to the broader narrative surrounding government involvement in UFO investigations.

David Grusch

However, in July 2023, United States Air Force (USAF) officer and former intelligence official David Grusch was interviewed by various media outlets and testified in a U.S. House of Representatives congressional hearing. Grusch claimed that he had conversations with unnamed officials that led him to believe that the U.S. federal government maintains a secretive UFO (or UAP) recovery program and is in possession of "non-human" spacecraft along with their "dead pilots". In 2022, Grusch filed a whistleblower complaint with the U.S. Office of the Intelligence Community Inspector General (ICIG) to support his plan to share classified information with the U.S. Senate Select Committee on Intelligence. He also filed a complaint alleging retaliation by his superiors over a similar complaint he made in 2021.

He claims to have viewed documents reporting that Benito Mussolini's government recovered a "non-human" spacecraft in 1933, which the Vatican and the Five Eyes assisted the U.S. in procuring in 1944 or 1945. Grusch claims second hand knowledge that American citizens have been harmed and killed as part of the government's efforts to cover up the information. In response to his June 2023 claims, the National Aeronautics and Space Administration (NASA) and the U.S. Department of Defense (DoD) issued statements reaffirming that no evidence of extraterrestrial life has been discovered and that there is no verifiable information about anyone possessing and reverse engineering any "extraterrestrial materials".

In July 2023 testimony given to the House Committee on Oversight and Accountability, Grusch repeated some of his claims under oath, alongside testimony from retired U.S. fighter pilot Ryan Graves and retired U.S. Navy commander David Fravor on their personal experiences related to UFOs. Grusch testified that he could not elaborate publicly on some aspects of his claims, but offered to provide further details to representatives in a sensitive compartmented information facility (SCIF).

David Charles Grusch is a decorated Afghanistan combat veteran and former Air Force intelligence officer who worked in the National Geospatial-Intelligence Agency (NGA) and the National Reconnaissance Office (NRO). From 2019 to 2021, he was the representative of the NRO to the Unidentified Aerial Phenomena Task Force. From late 2021 to July 2022, he was the co-lead for UAP analysis at the NGA and its representative to the task force. He assisted in drafting the National Defense Authorization Act of 2023, which includes provisions for reporting of UFOs, including whistleblower protections and exemptions to non-disclosure orders and agreements. Congressional interest in UFO sightings immediately prior to Grusch's public claims surrounded questions about the four objects that the Air Force shot down in February 2023.

Sean Kirkpatrick, director of the All-domain Anomaly Resolution Office tasked with investigating and reporting to Congress on UAPs

On June 5, 2023, independent journalists Leslie Kean and Ralph Blumenthal provided a story detailing Grusch's claims of a UFO cover-up by the government to The Debrief, a website that describes itself as "self-funded" and specializing in "frontier science". The New York Times and Politico declined to publish the story, while The Washington Post was taking more time to conduct fact-checking than Kean and Blumenthal felt could be afforded because, according to Kean, "people on the internet were spreading stories, Dave was getting harassing phone calls, and we felt the only way to protect him was to get the story out". According to Kean, she vetted Grusch by interviewing Karl Nell, a retired Army colonel who was also on the UFO task force, and "Jonathan Grey" (a pseudonym) whom Kean described as "a current U.S. intelligence official at the National Air and Space Intelligence Center (NASIC)". Kean wrote that Nell called Grusch "beyond reproach" and that both Nell and "Grey" supported Grusch's claim about a secret UFO retrieval and reverse engineering program. Also on June 5, portions of an interview of Grusch by Ross Coulthart aired on NewsNation with additional excerpts appearing on June 11.

Grusch claims that the U.S. federal government maintains a highly secretive UFO retrieval program and possesses multiple spacecraft of non-human origin as well as corpses of deceased pilots. Grusch also claims there is "substantive evidence that white-collar crime" took place to conceal UFO programs and that he had interviewed officials who said that people had been killed to conceal the programs. Grusch stated that he tried to get the director of AARO to help him share his claims with Congress, "I expressed some concerns to Dr. Kirkpatrick about a year ago, and told him what I was starting to uncover. And he didn't follow up with me."

Grusch elaborated on his claims in a subsequent interview with the French newspaper Le Parisien on June 7. He said that UFOs could be coming from extra dimensions; that he had spoken with intelligence officials whom the U.S. military had briefed on "football-field" sized crafts; that the U.S. government transferred some crashed UFOs to a defense contractor; and that there was "malevolent activity" by UFOs.

During a July 26, 2023, Congressional hearing, Grusch said that he "was informed in the course of my official duties of a multi-decade UAP crash retrieval and reverse engineering program to which I was denied access" and that he believes that the U.S. government is in possession of UAP based on his interviews with 40 witnesses over four years. Grusch claimed in response to Congressional questions that the U.S. has retrieved "non-human" biological matter from the pilots of the crafts and that this "was the assessment of people with direct knowledge on the [UAP] program I talked to, that are currently still on the program". When asked by U.S. Representative Tim Burchett during this July 26 hearing, if Grusch had "personal knowledge of people who've been harmed or injured in efforts to cover up or conceal" the government's possession of "extraterrestrial technology,"

Grusch said yes but that he was not able to provide details except within a SCIF.

BBC Radio 4's The World Tonight on August 3, 2023, interviewed Grusch along with his attorney Charles McCullough, a former Intelligence Community Inspector General. When asked about the U.S. having "intact and partially intact alien vehicles in its possession", Grusch repeated his claims, and McCullough noted that Congress should have "access to the information it needs to properly oversee things going on in the executive branch".

Joshua Semeter of NASA's UAP independent study team and professor of electrical and computer engineering with Boston University's College of Engineering concludes that "without data or material evidence, we are at an impasse on evaluating these claims" and that, "in the long history of claims of extraterrestrial visitors, it is this level of specificity that always seems to be missing". Adam Frank, a professor of astrophysics at the University of Rochester, published a critique of the Grusch claims on June 22 with Big Think. Frank writes that he does "not find these claims exciting at all" because they are all "just hearsay" where "a guy says he knows a guy who knows another guy who heard from a guy that the government has alien spaceships". Frank also said of the Grusch account that "it's an extraordinary claim, and it requires extraordinary evidence, none of which we're getting", adding "show me the spaceship".

The Guardian printed an opinion piece by Stuart Clark about Grusch's claims which included questions from three scientists. Harvard University astronomer Avi Loeb, who co-founded the UFO-investigating Galileo Project, noted that nothing extraterrestrial has been observed. Radio astronomer Michael Garrett noted that crashed landings of alien craft "would imply that there must be hundreds of them coming every day, and astronomers simply don't see them". Sara Russell, a planetary scientist from the Natural History Museum in London, said that, "if you give me an alloy, it would take me less than half an hour to tell you what elements are in it", and that "it should be easy to understand whether something falling to Earth is man-made or extraterrestrial, and if it is the latter, whether it is naturally occurring or not".

Greg Eghigian, a history professor at Pennsylvania State University and expert in the history of UFOs as it occurs in the context of public fascination, notes that there have been many instances over recent decades in the U.S. of people "who previously worked in some kind of federal department" coming forward to make "bombshell allegations" about the truth regarding UFOs with the whistleblower claims by Grusch fitting this pattern. Eghigian describes the 1940s–50s media enthusiasm about flying saucers, and comments that the successful books on the subject by authors Donald Keyhoe, Frank Scully, and Gerald Heard "provided the model for a new kind of public figure: the crusading whistleblower dedicated to breaking the silence over the alien origins of unidentified flying objects." Since then all these similarly credentialed claimants have been unable to provide any further corroboration. Eghigian said that "a new kind of sobriety needs to be interjected here" and that the Grusch story "ups the ante" but is "very hard to take seriously unless we start getting some real evidence that's of a forensic nature to prove these things".

Seth Shostak, the senior astronomer at the SETI Institute writing on MSNBC.com about Grusch's claims, said that the claims are extraordinary, before asking, "But where is the evidence? It's MIA. Neither Grusch nor anyone else claiming to have knowledge of secret government UAP programs has ever been able to publicly produce convincing photos showing alien hardware splayed across the landscape. And remember, we're not talking about a Cessna that plowed into a wheat field. We're talking about, presumably, an alien interstellar rocket, capable of bridging trillions of miles of space, and sporting technology that is obviously alien". Shostak concluded that, "from the standpoint of science, there's still no good evidence [that extraterrestrials are visiting the Earth], only an 'argument from authority'". Michael Shermer, publisher of Skeptic magazine, said of the July 26, 2023, congressional hearing that "it's astonishing it's come this far without any real evidence, without anybody in the scientific community making an appearance" and "we are still seeing not a shred of physical evidence".

Physicist and cosmologist Sean M. Carroll said of Grusch's claims about non-human visitors, "the evidence is laughable". About Grusch's physics claims, Carroll said that Grusch was "talking about the holographic principle and extra dimensions and stuff like that" which should "set off your alarm bells". He concluded that Grusch "has all of the vibes of a complete crackpot".

Laurie Leshin, Jet Propulsion Laboratory (JPL) director for NASA, when asked by reporter in August 2023 if she had "seen spacecraft made from outside of this world", replied "Absolutely not. No." with a laugh and head shake.

Physicist and popular science writer Michio Kaku told NewsNation that "so far we have not seen the smoking gun" to prove any of Grusch's claims. However, he also suggested that "the burden of proof has shifted, now the Pentagon has to prove these things aren't extraterrestrial". That prompted Real Clear Science editor Ross Pomeroy to comment, "no, the burden of proof has not shifted. Aliens are not the default explanation when a simpler explanation readily does the job". According to Pomeroy, "Kaku is seriously jeopardizing his reputation and misleading the public through his unscientific new stance on UFOs."

White House Press Secretary Karine Jean-Pierre referred questions about Grusch's complaint to the Department of Defense (DoD). In a statement, Sue Gough, spokesperson for the Pentagon, said: "To date, AARO (All-domain Anomaly Resolution Office) has not discovered any verifiable information to substantiate claims that any programs regarding the possession or reverse-engineering of any extraterrestrial materials have existed in the past or exist currently. AARO is committed to following the data and its investigation wherever it leads."

General Mark Milley, the chairman of the Joint Chiefs of Staff gave an interview to The Washington Times on August 6, 2023, and said that he never saw or heard of any evidence that would back up the claims made by Grusch regarding "quote-unquote 'aliens' or that there's some sort of cover-up program". Milley added that he was not that surprised that such ideas would circulate and be believed by some within an organization as large as the U.S. military.

NASA stated: "One of NASA's key priorities is the search for life elsewhere in the universe, but so far, NASA has not found any credible evidence of extraterrestrial life and there is no evidence that UAPs are extraterrestrial. However, NASA is exploring the solar system and beyond to help us answer fundamental questions, including whether we are alone in the universe."

In response to Grusch's claims, Representative Mike Turner, chairman of the House Permanent Select Committee on Intelligence, said, "every decade there's been individuals who've said the United States has such pieces of unidentified flying objects that are from outer space" and that "there's no evidence of this and certainly it would be quite a conspiracy for this to be maintained, especially at this level". Representatives Anna Paulina Luna and Tim Burchett were tasked with organizing a hearing in response to the Grusch claims on behalf of the House Oversight Committee. This took place on July 26, 2023.

Senator Lindsey Graham found the claims unreasonable, saying, "If we'd really found this stuff, there's no way you could keep it from coming out". Senator Josh Hawley said, "I'm not surprised, necessarily, by these latest allegations, because it sounds pretty close to what they kind of grudgingly admitted to us in the briefing". Some senators, though not concerned about Grusch's specific claims, were concerned that Congress might not have been briefed on special access programs. Senator Kirsten Gillibrand, who led a Senate hearing on UFOs in April

2023, said she intends to hold a hearing to assess whether "rogue SAP programs" existed "that no one is providing oversight for". Senator Marco Rubio, vice-chair of the Senate Select Committee on Intelligence said, "there are people who have come forward to share information with our committee over the last couple of years" with "first-hand knowledge" and that they were "potentially some of the same people perhaps" referred to by Grusch.

Following the July 26 hearing with Grusch as a witness, a bipartisan group of U.S. representatives called for the formation of a select committee on UAPs with subpoena power.

In July 2023, Senate Leader Chuck Schumer and Senator Mike Rounds lead a proposed 64-page amendment to the 2024 National Defense Authorization Act, called the UAP Disclosure Act 2023 that proposes wider access to records of UAP and federal government ownership of any "recovered technologies of unknown origin". The enrolled bill directs the National Archives to collect government documents about "unidentified anomalous phenomena, technologies of unknown origin, and non-human intelligence".

2023 House Committee Oversight and Accountability hearing

On July 26, 2023, Grusch testified before the United States House Committee on Oversight and Accountability, regarding his experiences and claims. House Representatives present included Tim Burchett and Anna Paulina Luna.

He did so alongside retired U.S. fighter pilots Ryan Graves and retired U.S. navy commander David Fravor. Fravor gave a first-hand account of his involvement in a 2004 incident released in the Pentagon UFO videos involving his fighter jet and a UFO, and Grusch repeated his previous claims under questioning from house representatives.

Representative Alexandria Ocasio-Cortez asked the three witnesses, "If you were me, where would you look?" regarding answers to UAP questions and evidence to validate his claims. Grusch replied, "I'd be happy to give you that in a closed environment. I can tell you specifically." Since the hearing, several lawmakers have said that they want to hear more from Grusch in a sensitive compartmented information facility (SCIF), however, according to Representative Burchett, officials have informed the lawmakers "that Grusch doesn't currently have security clearance to discuss the issues in a SCIF".

Following the July 26, 2023, Congressional hearing, AARO's director Sean Kirkpatrick wrote on his LinkedIn page that, "contrary to assertions made in the hearing", Grusch "has refused to speak with AARO" so that some details said to have been given to Congress had not been provided to his office and also that the hearing was "insulting …to the officers of the Department of Defense and Intelligence Community who chose to join AARO, many with not unreasonable anxieties about the career risks this would entail". Kirkpatrick was not, however, posting in an official capacity. A Pentagon spokesperson told reporters that the post was Kirkpatrick's "personal opinions expressed in his capacity as a private citizen," and declined to comment on the content of the post.

Connections to studies funded by Robert Bigelow, Keith Kloor writing for the Scientific American on August 25, 2023, draws a line from "these outlandish assertions" by Grusch "to the vast repository of so-called studies" funded over past years by Robert Bigelow. Kloor also points to the specific references to "a football field–sized UFO" showing up in one of the claims made by Grusch and in past claims by Bigelow.

Reporting on psychiatric treatment received by Grusch, Ken Klippenstein reported in The Intercept on August 9, 2023, that Grusch was twice committed after incidents in 2014 and 2018 that involved drunkenness and suicidal comments. Police records mentioned post-traumatic stress disorder (PTSD). After the 2018 incident Grusch was placed under an emergency custody order and transported to an ER.

A mental health specialist requested a temporary detention order, whereupon Grusch was transferred to Loudoun Adult Medical Psychiatric Services, an inpatient program in the Inova Loudoun Cornwall Medical Campus in Leesburg. The article in The Intercept noted that "Grusch's ability to keep his security clearance" despite this history "appears to contrast with the government's treatment of other employees".

Related to the June 11, 2023, broadcast of more Coulthart interview content, NewsNation included multiple voices, such as skeptical investigator Mick West. He was interviewed on June 8 and 11 and said, "I don't think what [Grusch is] saying is accurate" and that, while "it's possible he's believing what he's saying, it's an incredible story that really needs some actual verification".

British journalist Nick Pope, who previously ran the British Ministry of Defense "UFO Desk", initially expressed hope for confirmation or disconfirmation of Grusch's claims, but now that Grusch has lost his security clearance and there is still no "smoking gun" Pope says it is difficult to see how the claims could be confirmed. He added that while he was at the Ministry of Defense if the US government had acquired craft and bodies, "they didn't tell the UK."

Writing for The Atlantic on June 7, Marina Koren pointed out that the case fits a long pattern of previous unprovable claims and that, "so far, the best evidence [Grusch has] come up with, besides his own word, is the government's denial". Matt Laslo, writing for Wired on June 13, described the sympathetic hearing of Grusch's claims by some members of Congress as an indication that in "our strange new political universe of alternative facts turned dystopian reality, once-fringe notions have built-in fan bases in today's Capitol". Conservative political commentator Tucker Carlson gave publicity to the claims in a video posted to Twitter, and more recently a video in which he interviews David Grusch posted to YouTube. Tom Rogan, writing in the Washington Examiner on June 12, was skeptical regarding the extent of Grusch's claims, but said that they should be further investigated.

Outside the United States, the story received attention from multiple foreign mainstream news outlets, in such countries as Denmark, Germany, Austria, France, the Netherlands, Sweden, Norway, Croatia and Turkey. The 2023 House Committee hearing at which Grusch testified brought much wider coverage to his claims including major international outlets like the BBC, CNN and others.

Accusations of an intentional UFO disinformation campaign have been a feature of the coverage of this story. Grusch said intentional disinformation was being pushed by the US government to cast doubt on the veracity of "non-human" (or alien) claims such as his. Adam Gabbatt of The Guardian described Grusch's position as "a common conspiracy trope in the UFO community". Others have suggested a different sort of intentional campaign that fed Grusch disinformation about aliens to encourage the public to believe in the extraordinary claim of aliens and crashed ships for ulterior motives. Gareth Nicholson, editor for the South China Morning Post, explored some of the military and technological reasons for the purported existence of such a campaign, "the current UAP flap could be an attempt by the US military to engage in a disinformation campaign to disguise real aerospace breakthroughs or an attempt to flush out advanced technologies held by rivals such as Russia and China".

Andrew Prokop, a political news correspondent with Vox, wrote on 10th June 2023 that, "skeptics question whether Grusch is just repeating tall tales that have long circulated through the UFO-believing community, suggesting he may be just a gullible sap (if not an outright fabulist)." Prokop went on to state that, "mainstream media sources have so far remained wary of Grusch – The New York Times, Washington Post, and Politico were all offered his story but none thought it was publishable. The Debrief, which published it, is a notably UFO-friendly outlet, as are Leslie Kean and Ralph Blumenthal, the two journalists who wrote the story. And purported bombshells like this in the past have tended to fizzle out."

Sean Thomas expressed confusion in his opinion piece for The Spectator on June 24 that, preceding Grusch, there have been others trying to convince officials and the public that UFOs are worthy of serious considerations including some who themselves were high-ranking U.S. officials. The New York Times columnist Ross Douthat noted in a June 10 opinion piece that one interpretation of the flap is that parts of the U.S. government see benefit in promoting belief in UFOs, noting similarities between Grusch's claims and the claims of Garry Nolan, Stanford pathology professor and longtime proponent of the UFO extraterrestrial hypothesis, among others. According to Leslie Kean, Nolan knows and respects Grusch. In June 2023, Matt Stieb, writing for New York, described Grusch's claims in Coulthart's interview as "crazy".

Ezra Klein, a columnist with The New York Times, posted a podcast interview with Kean on 20th June, 2023, noting that "the main reactions" to her recent story about Grusch "have been to either embrace it as definitive truth or dismiss it out of hand." Klein asked a series of skeptical questions. Kean agreed that it is hard to imagine the government managing to keep programs secret for so long.

Documentary filmmaker and investigative journalist Steven Greenstreet criticized Grusch in a video with the New York Post for previously attending UFO conventions and associating with Skinwalker Ranch ufologists Jeremy Corbell and George Knapp, whom he met at a Star Trek Convention and both of whom sat behind Grusch at the 26th July Hearing and whom Representative Tim Burchett recognized from the dais and read their statements into the record.

The huge, explosive nature of Grusch's claims have divided opinions across a wide and diverse cross-section of society. Time will tell whether or not those claims are true.

CHAPTER SEVEN

Skepticism, Debunking, Truth & the Legacy

In the realm of skepticism and debunking, the Bonnybridge and Falkirk Triangle UFO encounters stand as intriguing case studies that have captivated both skeptics and believers alike. The incidents, which gained prominence in the late 20th century, center around the towns of Bonnybridge and Falkirk in Scotland, where numerous residents reported witnessing unusual and unexplained aerial phenomena, leading to the area being colloquially referred to as the Falkirk Triangle.

Skeptics, as their name implies, approach such reports with a critical lens, aiming to unravel the mysteries through logical and scientific means. In the Bonnybridge and Falkirk cases, skeptics contend that many of the reported sightings can be attributed to natural phenomena, misidentifications of conventional aircraft, atmospheric anomalies, or even psychological factors influencing perception.

One common skeptical approach is to analyze eyewitness accounts and scrutinize them for inconsistencies or alternative explanations. For instance, lights in the sky might be attributed to celestial bodies, military aircraft, or atmospheric conditions rather than extraterrestrial visitation. Skeptics also emphasize the role of cultural and psychological factors that can contribute to the misinterpretation of events, reinforcing the idea that a critical assessment is essential.

Despite the efforts of skeptics to debunk UFO sightings in the Bonnybridge and Falkirk Triangle, proponents of the unexplained phenomena argue that there are aspects that resist conventional explanations. Witnesses often describe sightings with remarkable consistency, detailing unusual flight patterns, speeds, and characteristics that defy known aircraft capabilities. Proponents stress the need for open-minded investigation and further scientific inquiry to explore the possibility of extraterrestrial involvement or other paranormal factors.

The ongoing debate surrounding the Bonnybridge and Falkirk Triangle UFO encounters illustrates the tension between skepticism and the acknowledgment of unexplained phenomena. It showcases the importance of maintaining a balanced perspective, recognizing the potential for both misinterpretation and genuine mysteries that may challenge our current understanding of the world.

Can we dismiss the 300 plus UFOs reports that come from Bonnybridge yearly? Billy Buchanan claims 60,000 people have seen UFOs in the Falkirk Triangle over the years he has been a local councilor. If true, that's a substantial number that should be taken seriously.

In this dynamic landscape of skepticism and belief, the Bonnybridge and Falkirk Triangle incidents serve as reminders that the pursuit of truth requires a nuanced approach. Whether through scientific scrutiny, eyewitness testimony analysis, or a combination of investigative methods, the interplay between skeptics and believers in these cases contributes to a broader dialogue on the nature of skepticism, debunking, and the exploration of the unknown.

In the pursuit of unraveling the Bonnybridge UFO enigma, researchers delve into the historical fabric of the region's UFO sightings. By meticulously scrutinizing records dating back decades, investigators aim to establish patterns, cross-referencing eyewitness accounts and discerning any recurring themes. The historical context serves as a crucial foundation, offering insights into the evolution of sightings and potentially uncovering factors influencing their occurrence.

Interviewing witnesses plays a pivotal role in the ongoing investigations. Beyond merely recording accounts, researchers employ psychological and forensic methodologies to assess the reliability and credibility of witnesses. Analyzing the emotional and psychological impact of the encounters provides a holistic understanding of the phenomenon. Witness testimonies not only contribute to the veracity of the investigation but also add a human dimension to the scientific exploration of these mysterious events.

The advent of sophisticated data analytics techniques enhances the systematic study of UFO sightings in Bonnybridge. Researchers employ statistical models to discern trends, identify outliers, and determine the statistical significance of observed patterns. By synthesizing data from multiple sources, including eyewitness accounts, sensor readings, and historical records, investigators gain a more comprehensive understanding of the nature of the phenomena, guiding further research directions.

The pursuit of truth extends to uncovering official responses and investigations carried out by governments. Researchers seek access to declassified documents that may shed light on the extent of governmental awareness and involvement in addressing the Bonnybridge UFO sightings. Analyzing bureaucratic responses and policy decisions provides a unique perspective on the official stance and the potential acknowledgment of the phenomena by authorities.

The modern arsenal of sensor technologies, including radar systems and advanced cameras, is deployed to capture precise data on UAP. These technologies facilitate real-time monitoring and recording of aerial events, allowing for more accurate measurements of speed, altitude, and trajectory. The integration of these cutting-edge tools contributes to the creation of a robust database, enhancing the scientific rigor of investigations.

Artificial intelligence and machine learning algorithms act as force multipliers in the analysis of vast datasets. These technologies autonomously sift through immense amounts of information, identifying complex patterns and anomalies that might elude traditional analytical methods. The synergy between human intuition and machine-driven insights amplifies the efficiency and effectiveness of the investigative process.

In recognition of the global nature of UAP phenomena, researchers increasingly collaborate on an international scale. This collaboration extends beyond traditional institutional borders, fostering a collective effort to pool resources, share methodologies, and validate findings. Simultaneously, public engagement initiatives leverage the power of crowdsourcing, with mobile apps and online platforms encouraging individuals to contribute their observations. This democratization of data collection broadens the research base, offering a diverse and inclusive approach to understanding the Bonnybridge UFO enigma.

As the search for truth unfolds, the synthesis of historical insights, witness testimonies, advanced technologies, and global collaboration contributes to a comprehensive exploration of the Bonnybridge UFO enigma. The evolving landscape of UAP research stands as a testament to humanity's collective curiosity and determination to unravel the mysteries that linger in our skies.

In the picturesque landscapes of Scotland, the quaint town of Bonnybridge has etched its name onto the canvas of the extraordinary, owing to a pervasive and enigmatic series of UFO sightings that have become synonymous with its identity. This otherworldly phenomenon, occurring with an unusual frequency, has woven a rich tapestry of narratives that reverberate through the annals of Bonnybridge's history, transcending the bounds of the unexplained.

The town's saga started in the early 1990s with a cascade of media coverage, as numerous eyewitness accounts of UFO sightings in and around Bonnybridge capture the collective imagination. Documentaries, television shows, and news articles delve into the mystique surrounding the town, chronicling its unique position as a celestial hotspot. This kaleidoscopic media panorama, alternately intriguing and unsettling, has not only lured the curious gaze of global audiences but has also subtly influenced the consciousness of the local residents, who find themselves living amidst the enigmatic.

The UFO legacy has permeated not only the town's physical landscape but also its cultural milieu. Bonnybridge's ethereal aura finds expression in literature, music, and art. Writers craft tales steeped in the enigma of the cosmos, while artists draw inspiration from the town's ethereal atmosphere, contributing to a unique cultural footprint that reverberates far beyond the boundaries of Bonnybridge.

The people of Bonnybridge, confronted with the extraordinary, have exemplified resilience in the face of uncertainty. The town's ability to transform potential unease into an opportunity for growth serves as a lesson for communities navigating unforeseen challenges. The resilience of Bonnybridge becomes a beacon, urging others to face the unknown with adaptability and determination.

Amidst the unexplained phenomena, Bonnybridge beckons the scientific community to unravel its mysteries. Lessons abound in the town's engagement with scientists, researchers, and experts, fostering a spirit of curiosity and exploration that extends beyond the immediate boundaries of Bonnybridge.

Despite the perplexities surrounding the UFO sightings, Bonnybridge's community finds unity in the face of the extraordinary. This sense of shared experience becomes a model for other communities confronting unique challenges, emphasizing the importance of solidarity when confronted with the unknown.

The legacy of Bonnybridge transcends mere tales of UFO sightings, becoming a nuanced narrative that weaves through the town's identity, permeating popular culture, commerce, and communal spirit. The UFO enigma in Bonnybridge stands as a testament to the profound impact that the unexplained can wield, encouraging communities to confront uncertainties with resilience, curiosity, and a collective sense of unity.

As Billy Buchanan says of the MoD and British Government: "We want answers."

Indeed we do…

ABOUT THE AUTHOR

My name is DJ Browne. I've been researching the so-called paranormal seriously since 1990. Before that, I had many unexplained encounters but like many people just shrugged and wrote them off. I have a significant archive of photographic, real time Direct Radio Voice/EVPs, and video evidence of the paranormal. For me, life is about celebrating the unexplained and so-called paranormal. The truth of reality and consciousness are stranger than we might at first believe. Experiencers the world over KNOW their truth is unique and potent. The only evidence you need is your own. Beyond the debate and ego, it really is very simple: Love and peace.

DJ Browne is the author of two books "Genuine Paranormal Research" and "UFOs Over Bonnybridge." He is working on an exciting third, as yet, un-named title.

Printed in Great Britain
by Amazon